SELF STUDY

SELF STUDY
Notes on the Schizoid Condition

DAVID KISHIK

ici
BERLIN PRESS

ISBN (Print): 978-3-96558-045-9
ISBN (PDF): 978-3-96558-046-6
ISBN (EPUB): 978-3-96558-047-3

To Imagine a Form of Life, v

Bibliographical Information of the German National Library
The German National Library lists this publication in the Deutsche
Nationalbibliografie (German National Bibliography); detailed
bibliographic information is available online at http://dnb.d-nb.de.

Cover design: Studio Bens, with a photograph by David Kishik, reflected in
Scott Lyall's *Talent*, courtesy of the artist and Miguel Abreu Gallery

In Europe, the paperback edition is printed by Lightning Source UK Ltd.,
Milton Keynes, UK. See the final page for further details.

The digital edition can be downloaded freely at:
https://doi.org/10.37050/hs-01.

ICI Berlin Press is an imprint of
ICI gemeinnütziges Institut für Cultural Inquiry Berlin GmbH
Christinenstr. 18/19, Haus 8
D-10119 Berlin
publishing@ici-berlin.org
press.ici-berlin.org

Contents

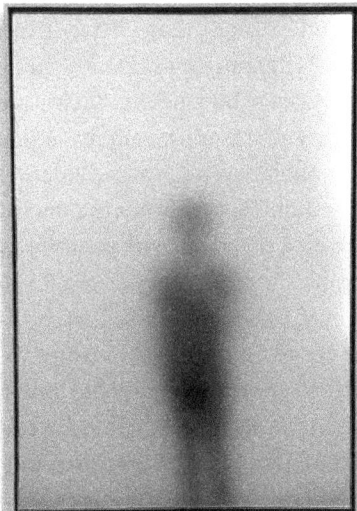

Figure 1.

1.   By filling one page each day in this empty notebook, I will write here mainly for myself and maybe also for some strangers. Rather than a diary revolving around my (boring) life and (insane) times, I see it turning into an *autophilosophy*. Wittgenstein said that working in philosophy is really working on oneself. Such a philosophy of myself, like every philosophy, cannot be dedicated to either private or public events, just as it cannot be labeled either fact or fiction. The aim is not to sketch a faithful self-portrait but to etch the surface of an entire mirror until it reflects only a blurry outline of me and my surroundings. These notes might also double as therapy sessions on a budget, since they will be less an attempt to imagine my form of life than to unravel it: they could unweave the fabric or disentangle the knots in preparation for a new fabric and the knots to come. So I first have to lose, not find, myself. The point is to exit, not enter, the monastery inside me. Auto-philo-sophy is therefore not the love of one's own wisdom, but the wisdom of one's love; which might sound sentimental, but it will soon reveal a darker truth. Hence a warning must be posted before I proceed: "If you want riches and old age, do not turn this very first page."

2.   Philosophy emerged from a basic yet elusive plea: *know thyself*. The idea was that humans cannot be moral without being selfish — not in the negative sense of lacking consideration for others, but in the positive sense of concerning oneself with oneself. In other words, life is not worth living unless you examine it. As Foucault demonstrates, the most elementary civic duty in an ancient democracy was the care of the self. So the Greek answer to the question *what is philosophy?* was already autophilosophy, which was always a practice or an activity, never a doctrine or an imperative. Autophilosophy was not a preparation for life but a form of life in and of itself, occupying the center of the classical cultural experience. A millennium later, this idea survived in Augustine's "I am working hard in this field, and the field of my labor is my own self. I have become a problem to myself." It reemerged after another millennium in Montaigne's "more than any other subject, I study myself. That is my metaphysics, that is my physics." Nevertheless, in the course of Western history, the philosophizing subject slowly faded away as the main subject of philosophy. Sometimes the self was renounced outright, while at other times it was quietly pushed aside by a variety of largely impersonal themes.

3.   Modern thought did not abandon the ancient interest in self-reflection, though it certainly redrew the target: a clear and distinct knowledge of the external world, which is possible only via an appeal to the inner self. "I will get into conversation with myself," Descartes writes, "examine myself more deeply, and try in this way to gradually know myself more intimately." But what is this self that serves as his ultimate fountain of certainty? A thinking thing? Nietzsche is not convinced: "We are unknown to ourselves, we knowers, and with good reason. We have never looked for ourselves, so how are we ever supposed to *find* ourselves?" The more professional philosophers became in the past century, the less they seemed to remember their original calling. But what keeps them up at night is probably, hopefully, still themselves. So do I care if people understand my philosophy, or whether they understand *me*? Augustine again: "Do not love to dwell in the building, but dwell in the builder." He has in mind the world and its creator; I see a thought and its thinker. But I suspect that the present attempt to comprehend myself is also a defense against the risk involved in letting others comprehend me on their own terms, in an environment beyond my literary control.

4.   Blumenberg describes the common philosopher as a person standing on safe land, analyzing a shipwreck as it unfolds at sea. To write an autophilosophy, by contrast, means that *I must be the shipwreck*. But it also means that I am the iceberg. And that every entry in this notebook is a message in a bottle dispatched from the lonely island on which I'm stranded. Yet despite all evidence to the contrary, this is not merely about me. Like Emerson, I assume that "the deeper the scholar dives into his privatest, secretest presentiment, to his wonder he finds this is the most acceptable, most public, and universally true." However, such truth doesn't have to be all-encompassing but only far-reaching. The personal is not only political; it can also become theoretical. Isn't philosophy ultimately a critique of life? Just as an automobile — this self-moving cart without a horse — can accommodate anyone occupying the driver's seat, a work of autophilosophy is designed for its potential readers, not only its actual author. It is a form that applies to lives other than my own. I hope I have something to offer here beyond my particular story. Although I am aware that this text's specificity is a crucial criterion by which it might one day be judged.

5.   Why write and rewrite what is only half-heartedly meant to be publicly read? Foucault again: "One must have within oneself a kind of book that one rereads from time to time." Hence these are all *notes to self*. A notebook can address no other. Handwriting these entries each morning, then revisiting and revising them for days after, is not directed at some printed result, or a new way of being me. It is an attempt to intensify my present existence, which often feels diminished. It is as if I have little air to breathe, while this autophilosophy lets me produce my own oxygen. But why do I desire to arrive at a detached view of my abstracted self? If this work purports to be a flame, am I more than its wick? Since these are not essays drawn from full-blooded experiences, would fragments discarded by a damaged life suffice? Although I want to express my emotions, all I can report back is a gradual loss of affect, plus a growing sense of isolation. Is this what medieval monks called *taedium vitae*, a weariness that arises not from life's burdens but from its crawling emptiness? Barthes: "To write by fragments: the fragments are then so many stones on the perimeter of a circle: I spread myself around: my whole little universe in crumbs; at the center, what?" Certainly not a solid self.

6.   Many years ago I made the following comment in a separate notebook I had been keeping: "Life is like a frozen lake. How can I build a home on thin ice?" Last week I was startled to come across a similar metaphor employed by Binswanger to describe his schizophrenic patient's desperate attempt to hold on to every straw, due to the fear that, with any step she takes, the ice might break. A secure existence means that a person has both feet firmly planted on the ground, confident of themselves and of the world. By contrast, many schizophrenics lack this "indisputable protection of existence from falling, sinking, breaking through into its abyss," which results in a being that is no longer quite there in the world, a naked life stripped of its previous form. Existing feels like flailing while falling. Winnicott describes a milder unstable situation as the fear of *falling forever* and *going to pieces*. Laing further defines a similar critical condition as *ontological insecurity*. But is anyone's existence truly secure? Mustn't we all hold each other lest we fall? This is the case not only when it comes to helpless babies but also to fully-functioning adults. Thicker ice is not yet terra firma. So why do I continue to let many relationships melt away and just keep to myself?

7.   Before moving on, it might be a useful exercise to pause and give a more banal answer to the question of who I am, as if it was a normal reflection in a polished mirror, or a bio, or an obit. Born in 1977 in the southern Israeli desert, I was raised in a small community in the northern Galilee hills. My father's family immigrated from Lebanon when he was a teenager; my mother's parents are Eastern European Holocaust survivors. Right out of high school I fell in love with Netta, my classmate, but soon after she left to study modern dance in New York. I stayed for the mandatory military service, though I also managed to take philosophy classes after hours at a university near my base. Three years later we both graduated, and I joined her in Manhattan. While she made a name for herself as a dancer and choreographer, I did my graduate work and submitted a dissertation on Wittgenstein. After teaching part-time at a local community college, I spent a couple of years in Berlin, and then returned stateside for a job at a private college in Boston. I still commute there once a week by train from the Lower East Side, where Netta and I have been living for the past two decades. We never had kids, but she did make some dances and I did write some books that do feel like something.

Figure 2.

8.   Here is an alternative account: "David Kishik went through his usual cleaning round at the cotton processing factory when his right arm got caught in one of the machines that began pulling him in. The other workers heard a terrifying scream and made every attempt to save him, but his body was slowly and fatally crushed before their very eyes." This is a translation of news reports about my grandfather and namesake. The accident occurred mere months after he moved his family from Beirut, the Paris of the Middle East, to Bat Yam, a dusty suburb south of·Tel Aviv. My father, the eldest of four, was attending a boarding school at the time on the outskirts of Jerusalem, where he met my mother. I was born eight years after this disaster. When I was ten, Moshe Farber, my maternal grandfather, a retired train conductor who lost most of his family to the Nazis, hung himself from a tree in the middle of an orchard. The effect of these traumas somehow constitute, or destitute, my own being. In a way, my factual biological birth is no more than a light intermezzo between these two tragic acts. Now I begin to make better sense of Ahmed's claim that "theory can do more the closer it gets to the skin," observing its scars just as Plato observed the stars.

9.   Do I need to demonstrate some transformation or progression in my personal narrative? Can these notes turn me into a different person? My full Hebrew name, דוד קישיק, happens to be a palindrome (I discovered it in the third grade, to my parents' surprise), which is one reason why a before-and-after logic applies to neither my life nor my work. It is basically the same from each direction you look. Li: "What one carries from one point to another, geographically or temporally, is one's self. Even the most inconsistent person is consistently himself." The minor dramas of my unremarkable autobiography can be no more than idiotic distractions (*idiotes* in Ancient Greece was a private person). For example, will it make any difference to discuss the various effects of the twists and turns of my evolving relationship with Netta? So I am sorry to disappoint no one, but this notebook is not the usual confession. The only conversion I aspire to achieve involves no eternal truth or higher being but, again, the turn of one's attention from world to self. The subject converts into his or her own object, gazing at his or her gaze, with no guilt or absolution, no anger or catharsis. My aspiration for this text is for it to become a philosophical selfie of sorts, rather than a conceptual dick pic.

10.   My tendency is to focus on one thing that turns the rest to noise from which I do my best to disengage. There is no middle ground between an embrace and a cold shoulder. For example, everybody pales in comparison to Netta. Almost any other relationship is dismissed as either superfluous or disappointing. Roy, my fairly close friend, once wrote in an angry email: "The critic is easily triggered in you when it comes to anything outside your inner sphere." Writing has a similar effect, turning other activities into meaningless idolatry from which I wish to divest myself. And there is only one contemporary thinker, Agamben, I really look up to, while others are often brushed off as misguided. Not only do I avoid academic associations like the plague, there is no alternative intellectual community to which I belong. As teachers, peers, and students come and go, I seem to belong to no world. With few interlocutors, with research that fails to partake in a viable discourse, my prolific publications are propelled by a kind of cruel optimism: the vague hope is to reach out to sympathetic readers, though in reality my studies are isolating me even further. Two decades of work in philosophy led to few human contacts. My *oeuvre* is both the cause and the effect of my loneliness.

11.   What am I to make of *To Imagine a Form of Life*, the series of books that I have been publishing since 2008? First, I must rename all of them. Volume one is *To Imagine a Language*, an austere examination of the axis around which Wittgenstein's evolving thought turns. Volume two is *The Coming Politics*, a fragmentary investigation of the unitary power behind Agamben's work. Volume three is *A Theory of a City*, an imaginary sequel to Benjamin's *Arcades Project*. Volume four is *On the Rest of the World*, a radical rereading of the beginning of Genesis. I used to take these texts to be my credo. Writing them felt like building my home's exterior walls, just as the present notes are like the shingles for its roof (as for the floor, I am still at a loss). Throughout this process I have lost track of Wittgenstein's warning: "You write about yourself from your own height. You don't stand on stilts or on a ladder but on your bare feet." Rereading the four installments from start to finish after the last one was released became a painful way to set fire to my trusted stilts and ladders. I saw the cracks in all the walls. What once passed as philosophy suddenly presented itself as pathology. I became the antagonist in my own story, questioning this life that I have imagined for myself.

12.   Can philosophy turn into what Preciado calls auto-vivisection, "an exercise in self-cutting, an incision into subjectivity"? Am I a case study? But of what? "Life, without feeling alive" is how Laing describes the schizoid position, which only now, while composing this mid-career self-survey, I am coming to recognize as my own: "This shut-up self, being isolated, is unable to be enriched by outer experience, and so the whole inner world comes to be more and more impoverished, until the individual may come to feel he is merely a vacuum." First the schizoid distances himself from an external life he deems desolate, especially when compared to the rich life he cultivates within. But after a while he "longs to get *inside* life again, and get life *inside* himself, so dreadful is his inner deadness." The irony is that my philosophical work has been an effort to affirm life and resist nihilism, to imagine a form of life rather than criticize it. By contrast, the schizoid ideal is a "will to nothingness, an aversion to life," to quote Nietzsche's not unrelated genealogy of the ascetic ideal, though in my case the subject who is doing the willing is often missing in action. Schizoid life is but a life sentence, served daily in the ordinary world. It is a life lost, and I'm it.

13.   Introverted, self-sufficient, withdrawn, unemotional, impersonal, distant, lonely: these are more common descriptors that came to be associated with a schizoid personality disorder since Bleuler introduced its first symptomatology. Alternately, I need to consider Kafka's "The Burrow," a story about an unidentified animal that digs an increasingly complex maze of underground tunnels to fend off an unspecified external threat. But the protagonist's belabored monologue led this exhausted reader to finally realize that the maze's protection is self-entrapment, that the unseen danger is made up, and that the subterranean abode is ultimately a grave. So I wonder whether my theoretical burrowing is meant to reveal my inner life to others and open myself to reality, or whether it ends up drawing a curtain that keeps me from being seen, and keeps me from seeing? Is my paranoid thought akin to a radar that scans the dark sky for malevolent intruders who do not exist? "A cage went in search of a bird" is how Kafka puts it in his personal notebook. Like a coconut, the schizoid's liquid core demands the hardest of shells. A practice of self-fencing is deemed necessary, which can deteriorate into self-bullying. Like Kafka's characters, Kafka himself, and so many others, I am mainly a victim of my own actions.

14.   Much of the study that led to this notebook was conducted in coffee shops around town. I alternated between a handful of different establishments, since I preferred to go unnoticed rather than be recognized as a regular customer. This tactic is taken to the extreme by one of Laing's schizoid patients: "Under the conviction that he was nobody, that he was nothing, he was driven by a terrible sense of honesty to *be* nothing. […] Being anonymous was one way of magically translating this conviction into fact. […] He belonged nowhere. He was going from anywhere to anywhere: he had no past, no future. He had no possessions, no friends. Being nothing, knowing nobody, being known by none, he was creating the conditions which made it more easy for him to believe that he *was* nobody." Similarly, as I dedicate my books to four forms of life while occupying what feels like a personal and interpersonal void, I cannot let go of Lukács's realization that life has no meaning in and of itself, but "only *in relation to something*, and this relation is meaningless and yet it completely absorbs the life — for a moment at least; but then life is made up of nothing but such moments." Even if I am just relating to myself, as I do in the present notebook, this consciousness is a small assurance that I still exist.

15.   Since social life not only requires but also builds an interpersonal immune system, schizoids can either feel infected while being with others, or suffer an autoimmune attack by themselves. So they tend to renounce needs and desires, treating the emptiness as an ideal of human existence. The self, by itself, feels that it deserves nothing. By practicing detachment, everything and everyone is met with a Bartleby-like silent resistance. The less one wishes, the safer one feels, the further one retreats, the harder it gets for others to break through the shell, which gets thicker every year. The more the world disappoints, the more appealing this strategy becomes. But the split (*skhizein* in Greek) between inner self and outer world is more than the subject's adequate reaction to a particular bad object. It inevitably becomes a relentless mode of being, as a patina of futility begins to settle over everything. Hence the antisocial-oppositional stance can often give way to a passive-compliant one. Like mice, the schizoid tactic is to timidly venture out and then quickly retreat back in to regroup. Like Schopenhauer's porcupines, the dilemma is that by staying close together they sting each other, while at a distance they freeze. Schizoids are desperate for love, but they also desperately fear it.

16.   My dad is a devoted player of a solitaire card game on his desktop computer, to which he dedicates at least an hour every day. We once had an odd phone conversation in which we speculated on life at the end of days. He suggested that the saved might also play solitaire for eternity. When I wondered whether they could play a different game that would allow them to interact with one another, he replied that my suggestion was far from ideal, since it would inevitably create winners and losers. Like father, like son: writing is my solitaire, even though I make it public. In my eyes, a finished book remains a personal notebook. Winnicott made me see that although a text arises from an urge to communicate, I am ultimately propelled, even in these tell-all entries, by the wish to never be found. Kretschmer was the first to describe these "shut-in" or "autistic" tendencies that are so prevalent among schizoids: "They close the shutters of their houses, in order to lead a dream-life" that stays "within the soft muffled gloom of the interior." You can knock, but no one is home. This desire to disengage is also present in the experience of the expatriate. Like my dad, I also left my childhood's landscape and language, culture and people. Unlike him, I now feel a bit foreign both here and there.

17.   After the preliminary psychiatric groundwork laid in the first decades of the twentieth century by Bleuler and Kretschmer, a peculiar character made its hesitant entrance into the West's intellectual stage. For about thirty years, from 1940 to 1970, *homo schizoid* came to the fore in the writings of Fairbairn and Guntrip, two psychoanalysts who are barely known today outside the professional circles that still adhere to their theoretical principles. During those decades, the figure of the schizoid also played a key role in the thought of Klein and Winnicott, as well as in Laing's *The Divided Self*, which introduced it to a larger audience. By now, this figure is all too often either forgotten or, even worse, confused with its psychotic relative, the schizophrenic. Yet my notebook is not simply haunted by the specter of this obscure mental aberration, nor is it merely a frank testimony of a twenty-first-century schizoid man. On a good day, when I don't just want to disappear, I sense that the stakes are much higher, that the schizoid condition is affecting this world in mysterious ways. Or is the attempt to generalize and de-emotionalize my personal and marginal pain by turning it into a grand theory of everything just another semi-shrewd coping mechanism?

18.   Fairbairn and Guntrip's groundbreaking thought begins with the experience of an unsatisfying and hence frustrating interpersonal relationship, which can lead to a feeling of either anger or hunger. "When you cannot get what you want from the person you need," Guntrip writes, "instead of getting angry you may simply go on getting more and more hungry." For Fairbairn, *love made hungry* is at the core of the schizoid experience. The problem, however, is that schizoids find love hard to metabolize. Their resulting social malnutrition, or self-starvation, makes it difficult to further digest meaningful relations, which are often substituted by shallow connections that give instant gratification but little nourishment, like much of online life. Even inanimate objects, consumed or hoarded, can pretend to replace the demands of human intimacy and hence act like temporary barriers protecting the individual from such vital demands. While anger and aggression lead one to first feel guilty and then depressed, schizoid withdrawal leads one to feel *nothing*. If hate becomes destructive it is still possible to love someone else. But if love seems destructive, if love is renounced, then there is no exit strategy. True hell is the life of a person who cannot shake off this conviction that hell is other people.

19.   The love a schizoid person both gives and receives is kept in a cage (because it is deemed too dangerous) or a safe (because it is too precious). The opposite of such love is not hate. "Hate is love grown angry because of rejection," Guntrip explains, since "we can only really hate a person if we want their love." The true opposite of both love and hate is *indifference*, which is the essential schizoid mood: "having no interest in a person, not wanting a relationship and so having no reason for either loving or hating." While narcissists need to be seen and get constant approval from others (though vitriol might also do), schizoids would much prefer to disappear. They tend (or pretend) to not care about both positive and negative feedback. To substitute for their failed relations with the external world, they construct and engage with an elaborate universe of internal objects. They dig their escape tunnel with a teaspoon. What such schizoids mainly care about is personal integrity and a claim for originality, with little attention to whether it is challenged by others. Their inner experiences encase them in a cold and closed system that slowly dims the light coming from their outer reality. Consuming a diet of self-involved ideas, they foreclose any possibility of being consumed by love that involves others.

20.   When human beings feel abandoned, they often deploy a mechanism Fairbairn calls the *moral defense*. Imagine a mother who broke her young daughter's arm. The abused child will usually convince herself (and anyone who asks, such as a nurse) that it happened because she was being bad. Otherwise she would have to face a disturbing truth about her mother that is too hard to bear. Put otherwise, "it is better to be a sinner in a world ruled by God than to live in a world ruled by the Devil." Fairbairn sees this bind as the source of the original split: God, like the parent, must be wholly good, while the child, like humanity (at least since Augustine), pretends to take the full blame. This is the standard way to explain how one becomes the schizoid one is. Another way, which I witnessed while eavesdropping on a young couple arguing in a shuttle bus to the Athens airport, illustrates an adjacent mechanism. At a moment's notice, the woman's agitation switched from panic to lifelessness. It was as if she shut herself off. Her eyes glazed over and her body turned into stone, while her partner couldn't get through to her as much as he tried. Was she hoping to disappear, to be unseen? Is it like kids who hide by closing their eyes? Why has one forsaken one's self? Am I afraid of living more than dying?

21.   I take the *immoral* defense to be another schizoid method to deal with this debilitating predicament. Personally, I withdraw from my environment because I subconsciously presume it will somehow contaminate or hurt me. But Žižek is actually right: "evil resides in the very gaze that perceives evil all around itself." Just as the moral defense blocks the incorporation of an external evil by concocting an internal one, the constantly critical stance of the immoral defense blocks the evil within by claiming it lies without. I dig a burrow to protect myself from an immoral world, even if deep down I know that it is the other way around, that I actually protect the world from a bad person. This defense ensures that my harmful proclivities remain unacknowledged, which is why every faux pas feels like a moral slip of the tongue, a small shameful reminder of my constant ability to hurt. Before evil is radical or banal it is liable to be relational. Whether I attack the world or the world attacks me, even if it is just a micro-aggression, the result is the same pressing need to erect a thick wall between the two. Surely, *the world* is always *other people*, which is why *amor mundi* is such a slippery proposition. Still, I somehow manage to both suffer and benefit from this schizoid split.

22.   The terms of the *schism* can vary — good and evil world, true and false self, inner and outer reality, relational and vegetal life, subject and object, mind and body, nature and culture — because homo schizoid is a machine that produces every dualistic division under the sun, as a direct reaction to psychic stress. Hegel already sensed that "I am twofold within myself," that self-consciousness arises from facing an other who is my negation. But it was Fairbairn who ultimately affirmed that "everybody without exception must be regarded as schizoid." This bold claim rings true to the extent that "the fundamental schizoid phenomenon is the presence of splits in the ego; and it would take a bold man to claim that his ego has so perfectly integrated" into an undivided whole. No one is an in-dividual, in the literal sense of being *indivisible*. The disturbances that result from the artificial and changeable conditions of the human species might be enough to splinter each and every psyche. As good as it gets, our nurture always fails us to some degree. If the resulting distress leads to fissions that make some of us cancel external relations and live a detached life, then it becomes difficult to challenge or change our divided selves. The more isolated I get, the more entrenched my splits become.

23.   Despite all the talk about loneliness as a public health crisis, rarely is there a discussion of the basic schizoid issue, of which loneliness is often no more than a symptom, as in my case. But am I lonely or do I just feel empty? Guntrip shows how compromised infantile care can lead an adult to feel "stranded in an impersonal milieu, a world empty of any capacity to relate to him," which leads to "the worst of all psychopathological states, the schizoid condition of withdrawn isolation, fundamental loneliness, profoundly out of touch with his entire outer world; so that people seem like 'things' and the material world around him seems like a flat unreal imitation." Because a human being becomes what it is through relations with external persons, being deprived of them is in some sense a mental suicide. It all starts when a subject's trust is breached. From then on, everything slowly retreats into an extensionless point until the solipsist is convinced of being utterly alone. At times, sex only perpetuates the loneliness it desperately tries to ameliorate. Schizoid life is self-inflicted social death, even under the confident disguise of a stoic existence. But while Guntrip tries to penetrate this hopeless core of loneliness, I still think of it as the philosopher's condition of work and preferred way of life.

24.   I've come to see philosophy as a socially-sanctioned schizoid vocation, and the best available record of the ontologically insecure mindset. An entire tradition perpetuates its own sense of spiritual superiority by unsettled practitioners, who at least give clear expression to a pathology that nonphilosophers usually manage to stave off. That virtually all philosophy is conducted today within the protective confines of the academy — another institution that reinforces rather than shuns schizoid behavior — literally adds insult to injury. That the genesis of both philosophy and the academy is associated with Plato is no coincidence. Kierkegaard said that, with Socrates, philosophy was "still just a life." But reading through Plato's voluminous opus makes it clear that he couldn't spend much time in actual conversations with the living. He had to be mainly by himself to write his imaginary dialogues. Witnessing his master betrayed by the Athenians and sentenced to death was a trauma that determined Plato's relationship with the world at large. His schizoid reaction to this tragic act of abandonment was to turn philosophy either inwards or upwards, but definitely away from what many philosophers still perceive as their false, cruel, or shallow earthly surroundings.

25.   Being with others is being vulnerable. Your ideas get tested, your pride punctured, over and over again. Socrates's irony subverted the tendency of the Athenian citizens to withdraw into a collective bubble of self-regard. He poked others, and others poked him. (Today I seem to sense in my students how living online makes it difficult for them to face me, and each other, in real life.) But when Plato first heard Socrates's voice — which lured him to switch from a career in theater to one in philosophy — the flight or exile from the world was already at work. Kierkegaard also said that even when Socrates told people, *know yourself*, he basically told them, *separate yourself from the other*. Nietzsche adds that Socrates was sick before he drank the poison, that something in him was indeed corrupting the youth, that the Athenians did have a point in demanding his elimination. In other words, the schizoid character of philosophy has been there from the get-go. Still, the inherent indeterminacy of a real relation with another person — like the one between Socrates and Plato, or Netta and me — means that this experience can never be reduced to a systematic argument or a rational theory, to a dualism or a dialectics. What is a book if not a tomb for a relationship? A good work is all too often a symptom of a lousy life.

26.   While I'm convinced that it is possible to detect schizoid traits in virtually every figure and doctrine from the history of philosophy, nowhere is this link more obvious than in the Stoic tradition. It can be found in the withdrawal from reality prescribed by Epictetus: "When you close your doors and create darkness within, remember never to say that you're on your own, for in fact, you are not alone, because God is within you, and your guardian spirit too. And what need do they have of light to see what you're doing?" Deleuze claims that, rather than swapping the outer for the inner, the Stoics actually want to stay on the *surface*, since even depth is devalued. Like good schizoids, they strive for *apatheia*, or lack of disturbing emotions, since these are beyond one's control. Thus Cicero wants "the happy man to be safe, impregnable, fenced, and fortified," while Marcus imagines him "like the rock that the waves keep crashing over." The oracle told Zeno that, to make the world disappear in the pursuit of the good life, he must join his flesh with that of the dead. "Seeing what this meant, [Zeno] read the works of the ancients," who, being dead, could not challenge the Stoics' founding father, conveniently enough. But who would want to be removed from the living by thinking?

27.   In retrospect, I don't think I ever felt more alive than I did that night I spent in the Tombs, the municipal jail in downtown Manhattan, after getting caught leaving a chain bookstore with an unpaid copy of *The Phenomenology of Spirit*. This incident from my student days reminds me of a line from Kojève's lectures on Hegel's book: "Man abandons Stoicism because, as a Stoic, he is *bored*. The Stoic ideology […] prevents Man from acting: it obliges him to be content with *talking*." But what is the *Phenomenology* at the day's end other than an uninterrupted monologue? All the discussions in it happened long before its author began his work. The evolving truth surveyed in his solitary and impersonal glide through the history of thought is freed from the external world outside his window. So instead consider an earlier challenge to the schizo-Stoic logic, which can be found in Pascal's posthumously published personal notebook: "Our happiness must be sought outside ourselves. Our passions drive us outwards, even without objects to excite them. External objects tempt us in themselves and entice us even when we do not think about them. Thus it is no good philosophers telling us: withdraw into yourselves and there you will find your good."

28.   The object sought by the ideal philosopher is supposedly called *wisdom*. But this love of wisdom can also easily stand in the way of real people. For example, in *The Consolation of Philosophy*, Boethius confesses to a relationship with an imaginary woman who stands for his philosophical pursuit. Apparently, she can console the fragile narrator where actual humans have failed. Luckily, I fell in love with Netta some months before I committed myself to philosophy. As an adult, these cerebral and romantic attachments alternately held me and made me feel safe. Otherwise, the temptation to use my rarefied vocation as an exclusive surrogate life partner would have been harder to resist. For the traditional philosopher, eternal or universal truths are comforting substitutes for persons who are unwilling to offer their unconditional love. Relations are always messy, and the philosopher is not always right. Hence Nietzsche suggests that "the philosopher abhors marriage," which is a "calamity on his path to the optimum." The philosopher "does *not* deny 'existence', he rather affirms *his* existence and *only* his existence." His prayer — "let the world perish, but let there be philosophy, the philosopher, *me!*" — presents the limit case where autophilosophy turns into autoerotic asphyxiation.

29.   Up to now philosophers have either interpreted or changed the world. How about simply *relating* to it? To imagine a relational turn in philosophy, following the one in psychoanalysis, is to judge a philosophical book by its ability to facilitate better connections between its readers and their surroundings — because philosophy tends to have the exact opposite effect, separating people from the world and from each other. What if the value of philosophers was measured by their ability to relate not only to other philosophers, but also to nonphilosophers? Or is it enough to develop fruitful connections between different thinkers and their disparate thoughts? This is not a Platonic love that strives for an ultimate intimacy with some divine truth or beauty. The intellectual love I am interested in is a bit like the love between an experienced couple, filled with frustrations and compromises. But it is usually unrequited and rarely monogamous: why love only one thinker, or expect reciprocation? For me, thinking about Wittgenstein and Agamben were exercises in fostering such relations, which are rarely personal, although I was on friendly terms with Agamben while writing *The Coming Politics*. Still, the notion that the only good philosopher is a dead one is pretty compelling.

30.   Not only philosophy but any job that rewards its practitioners for dissociating themselves from the external, shared world, while immersing themselves in an internal, imaginative, and impersonal one, inevitably draws into its ranks individuals with schizoid tendencies. It is something I wished I at least knew when I first got caught in this web two decades ago. An excellent illustration of this apparatus of capture, as well as a possible line of flight from it, is Piper's *Food for the Spirit*, a delicate piece of performance art she made while still a graduate student in philosophy. Dedicating the entire summer of 1971 to the study of Kant's first *Critique*, she rarely left her apartment. At times she had to stand in front of her mirror just "to make sure I was still there." Whenever she was overcome by "the fear of losing myself," she went back to her specular reality check. She then began taking pictures of her reflection in various stages of undress. Having an objective record of her physical appearance became a coping mechanism in her confrontation with a philosophical system that drove her to a state of "self-transcendence." The supposed universality of her pure reason was thus reminded of the boundaries of her individual self, its sex, its race, and other material conditions of her mental states.

31.   Guntrip considers the schizoid philosopher to be a particularly important type: "Highly abstract philosophy seems unwittingly designed to prove Descartes's dictum, *cogito ergo sum*, the perfect formula for the schizoid intellectual's struggle to possess an ego. A natural human being would be more likely to start from *I feel, therefore I am*. Even the schizoid person can become rapidly convinced of his own reality for the time being by feeling angry, whereas his thinking is usually a not very convincing struggle to hold on to a somewhat desiccated personal reality." Modern philosophy begins with a sham declaration of ontological security made by a man in seclusion whose sole interaction involves an imaginary evil genius, with a dualistic self irrevocably split into a mind and a body, with a subject who doubts every object that could give him a sense of certainty by simply relating to it in everyday life. Left to his own schizoid devices, Descartes is unable to foreclose the truth Hume discovered a century later, Buddhists knew for centuries before, and those who consume psychedelic drugs experience today: the self is no more than a bundle of perceptions, like a flame or a stream. Even in the short *cogito* it might remain inconstant: I (subject) think, therefore I (object) am.

32.   Working on *A Theory of a City* made me realize that the question *what is philosophy?* is best answered by further asking *where is philosophy?* Since Socrates, philosophy likes to present itself as a public practice, though the thinker is usually found at home, either symbolically or actually. Philosophers are private intellectuals long before a few of them vie for public attention, sometimes to disastrous effect. Philosophy is actually a kind of interior design put on public display — a house tour, as it were. I can enter some philosophers' space by engaging with their work, but I must remember that this is *their* mental space. I can pay a visit, but I can't move in for good, even if I were the foremost expert on their thought. But can I comfortably inhabit my own books as rooms of my own? And what about my physical space? From my teenage bedroom in Israel to my adult apartment in New York and my faculty office in Boston, I've developed a slight obsession with controlling their minimalist decor, maybe to minimize my attachment, or to express how little sparks joy in me. It is as if I barely live in the places I inhabit. These inner spaces, real or imagined, filled with a careful selection of objects and concepts, end up being my holding cells, where I feel compelled to stay put.

33.   In her penultimate notebook, Weil writes: "Humility is the acceptance of social death." In the last notebook she explains: "The connection between humility and true philosophy was known in antiquity. Among the Socratic, Cynic, and Stoic philosophers it was considered part of their professional duty to put up with insults, blows, and even slaps in the face without the slightest instinctive reaction of offended dignity." The humility of philosophy seems to go hand in hand with Weil's theology of creation, as both are suffused with disturbing schizoid thoughts: "For God, the creation consisted not in extending himself but in withdrawing […] the creation is an abandonment. In creating what is other than himself, God necessarily abandoned it." The only thing God still cares about is therefore the uncreated part of every creature. So to participate in the creation of the world, philosophers are asked to somehow *decreate* their selves. A philosopher in Weil's image knows that to say *I* is inevitably to lie. Inspired by her thought while writing *On the Rest of the World*, it first occurred to me that to do philosophy is to undo the philosopher, who is left to patiently, fixedly, and hopelessly contemplate insoluble problems in a state of humiliating withdrawal from an abandoned world.

34.   Again, I cannot think of any significant chapter in the history of Western metaphysics that is not touched by the schizoid logic. In my mind, Agamben represents the end of this line. "We are together and very close," he writes, "but between us there is not an articulation or a relation that unites us. We are united to one another in the form of our being alone." Hence he gestures toward a politics that is no longer based on the relation between individuals, and an ethics that stops relying on recognition between subjects. To achieve this unlikely goal, he deploys a method that does not embrace one position and reject the opposing one, but prefers to maintain a kind of *indifference* toward both. It leads him to view the human as a being who suspends "the immediate relation of the animal with its environment," who is the site of "ceaseless divisions and caesurae," who never ceases being an infant. Once again we meet here the figure of homo schizoid and not only that of homo sacer, as Agamben calls the obscure protagonist of his investigations. A work that begins with a study of the notion of banishment ends by abandoning not this or that relationship but the very idea of relationality, by imagining a life that can never be separated from its schizoid form.

35.   That Agamben was born on the same date as
my father and Wittgenstein shares his birthday with my
mother makes my early attempts to wrestle with their
thoughts all the more obvious. Yet behind this astrological
anecdote I now find a better explanation for my two
decades of attraction to these two thinkers. Unlike my
quick sketch of Agamben's schizoid position, Sass's well-
documented analysis traced the same schizoid pathology
throughout Wittgenstein's life and work. "One can always
withdraw into the self," Wittgenstein wrote in a coded
notebook as a young soldier. "Be sure not to be dependent
on the external world." However, I've never been satisfied
by an Oedipal gesture toward my philosophical parents.
My current task is neither to jettison anything touched
by schizoid symptoms nor to embrace the long-lasting
schizoid tradition as a rediscovered redemptive truth.
After wavering between these two rigid attitudes, I'm
realizing that this split into an entirely bad object of
critique and a wholly good emancipatory object is another
clear sign of what Fairbairn already called the moral
defense. For me, the schizoid must be both. It is a way
of thinking, living, and feeling that can neither be fully
affirmed nor totally negated while its palpable impact is
being reckoned with.

36.   Fairbairn and Guntrip's way of thinking is not anti-Oedipal, as Deleuze and Guattari's is, but *ante*-Oedipal. With Klein, they focus on the infantile condition that precedes the child's later contention with the parents. For Guntrip, "schizoid problems represent a flight from life, Oedipal problems represent a struggle to live." A secret desire to bed mommy and kill daddy is real progress for those who desire nothingness. For Fairbairn, the schizoid structure, not Freud's Oedipal complex, is humanity's most inescapable force. An *object* for Freud is the target of drives that are either sexual or violent in nature. Drives are innate, basically uncontrollable, and often dangerous energies. They require education, socialization, and even therapy to keep them in check. In Freud's theory, the drive comes first, and then the subject who contains it latches on to this or that object to get some relief. The focus is therefore on the individual as a discrete entity, divorced from its interpersonal context. The external environment is imposed on distinct persons for their own protection. This Freudian stance cannot integrate Winnicott's quintessential realization that there is no such thing as a baby (separate from its caregiver), that in the beginning was a relation.

37.   I think of an *object* as whatever a subject relates to, and a *subject* as whatever relates to an object. Both terms usually stand for actual people who have feelings toward each other, like Netta and me. Hence Guntrip's summary of what came to be known as *object relations theory*: at bottom, *we seek persons, not pleasures.* The aim in life is not to release tensions but to establish relations. Pleasure for pleasure's sake is often a way to mitigate my failure to get what I truly want. Without relying on the notion of the drive, Fairbairn argues that, above all, we are guided by the reality principle: by other humans and their vicissitudes. Pleasure (like pain) is *not a principle but a signpost* that gives directions on the way to the basic libidinal end: being with others. Hence, the definitive account of this psychoanalytic paradigm shift describes two divergent dramas: on Freud's stage, my life is ruled by the "inherent opposition among instinctual aims and between instinctual aims and social reality"; on Fairbairn's stage, I play the role of a person whose central problem is an inability to "maintain the integrity and wholeness of his experience of himself within his necessary relations with others, and is forced to fragment himself" in order to keep these relations alive.

38.   Fairbairn's priorities are radically different from Freud's: splitting eclipses repressing, the schizoid position upstages a depressive position, and schizophrenia overshadows melancholia. Yet Fairbairn's revolution was a soft one, partly because he was an outsider with few contacts in the psychoanalytic community. Not only studying but also personifying the schizoid life, he never bothered to found a school. Guntrip, his one devoted follower, was also his patient (after Fairbairn died, Winnicott became Guntrip's analyst). Fairbairn's far-reaching influence emanates from a limited number of rather dry and technical papers. His last publication is a two-page synopsis of his theory in seventeen pithy theses. It begins: "1. Ego is present from birth. 2. Libido is a function of the ego. 3. There is no death drive; and aggression is a reaction to frustration or deprivation. 4. Since libido is a function of the ego and aggression is a reaction to frustration or deprivation, there is no such thing as an *id*. 5. The ego, and therefore libido, is fundamentally object-seeking." If life's telos is good relations, death drive and id are for Fairbairn misnomers for a variety of largely destructive schizoid mechanisms that respond to our primordial anxiety, which is separation anxiety.

39.　　To elucidate this disruptive move, consider the not-so-hypothetical case of a man who joins a dating site for the sole purpose of finding women willing to meet him for one-night stands. The interactions he has, digitally and in person, are only obligatory means leading to the sexual end. There are times when almost no words are exchanged. Identities are rarely revealed. Pictures do most of the work. Meetings may recur as long as their purely physical nature is maintained. Whenever emotions are introduced or strings get attached, the relation is immediately terminated. Then the search for a new partner resumes, following an identical pattern, ad infinitum. To take the man's mind off this practice, he gets consumed by another type of online hunt: shopping for bargains. Freud would focus the analysis on the subject who fails to control his inner drives, while the women he lures and the deals he scores would stay in the background as the interchangeable objects of his perverse desire. Fairbairn would hold on to these superficial relations as a springboard for understanding the much more significant and much more problematic relationships that failed this man throughout his life, from the parents who once raised him all the way to the therapist who is currently talking to him.

40.   Swayed by thermodynamics, Freud's psycho-dynamic theory is ruled by an artificial split between energy and structure. Fairbairn's thought emerged from his realization that "both structure divorced from energy and energy divorced from structure are meaningless concepts." The convenience of the distinction between the two is not enough to make it true. In Freudian psychoanalysis we are asked to accept "a set of energyless structures (the ego) and a pool of structureless energy (the id)." The psychic apparatus supposedly operates like a car engine (subject) that cannot reach its destination (object) without some fuel (libido). In Fairbairnian psychoanalysis, by contrast, "there is no separation of ego from id. There is no pool of directionless energy which becomes secondarily oriented toward objects. Ego structures have energy—*are* energy—and that energy is structured and directed toward objects from the start." Put in slightly different terms, here lies what I find to be the most convincing argument for the inseparability of life from its form, for the impossibility to imagine either a formless life or a lifeless form. To think otherwise is the height of schizoid delusion, and the source of ethical and political disasters, not to speak of philosophical and aesthetical dead ends.

41.   Does the infant's failure to maintain a sense of omnipotence indeed lead to a growing grasp of reality? What if the failure of reality (poor caregiving) results in a child (and then an adult) who cultivates the pretense of being omnipotent (as a defense against a pervasive feeling of helplessness)? Are babies really driven by an incestuous desire for the mother's erotic pleasure? What if their existential fear of obliteration makes them search for safety by returning to her womb? Guntrip depicts the schizoid drama as a constant struggle to *stay born*, to stay alive. It is a fight against the forces of regression: the dream of an undifferentiated, prenatal stage, when subject and object were one, before all the splits. As the Greeks used to say, the best thing in life is not to be born at all. The flight from life into the security of the womb, this unattainable pre-relational state of not-yet-being-in-the-world, can manifest itself as a simple death wish. If life is a relation, then death literally *do us part*. Its twin fantasy is to be reborn into a less contentious environment. Those who are moved by such considerations may prefer not to leave their home and just stay in bed, as my mother used to do for long stretches of time. Home, for my purposes, is *where the world is not*.

42.   The last time my mom visited me in New York she brought some rags that she wore one morning to fulfill a longstanding dream of becoming homeless for a day. Without telling anyone about her plan, she walked to Chinatown and begged on a street corner. After a few hours, she gave whatever she collected to a real homeless person and returned to my apartment. She was so excited about her experience, but I was less enthusiastic. Being homeless and being homebound are both scenarios that trigger in me mild dread. Indoors I get trapped in my empty solitude and numbing comfort. Out in the street I am prone to self-deprivation or self-desertion (not buying myself food, not protecting myself from the elements). But the more I think about it, the less I am interested in tracing my schizoid tendencies back to their origin in some dormant prelinguistic maternal experience. Etymologically, *infancy* means *speechlessness*. Without speaking there can be no subject, who becomes one by saying *I*, by enunciating oneself in language. And without a subject, how can there be any proper experience of an object? Even if a breakdown that results in agony occurred during infancy, Winnicott insists that "this thing of the past has not happened yet because the patient was not there for it to happen to."

43.   How can one remember a trauma that, at least subjectively, did not really happen? For example, an unanswered call for help, which led the caller to feel empty. For Winnicott, to say that there is nothing to experience means that *there is a nothing* that must be experienced. But can one also *speak* of this nothingness, or must one remain silent? Language usually shields us from the truth of our infantile bareness, where communication begins and ends with a cry. So is therapy primarily about interpretation (with words) or about relation (over time)? A reply is encapsulated in a couple of pertinent details about the myth of Oedipus that were repressed by its psychoanalytic appropriation. The first, of course, is that Oedipus was abandoned at birth by his biological parents. The second is that, as an adult, he was the only person who solved the riddle of the Sphinx. Agamben suggests that Oedipus's original sin was neither patricide nor incest, but cracking this sacred enigma. He was desecrating a spiritual concealment by turning it into plain speech. It is the act of a heretic, not a hero. The Greeks never took the Sphinx lightly; any encounter with it came with the risk of death. And just like Oedipus, Freud wanted to say the unsayable, interpreting the secret at our *incommunicado* core.

44.   "Rape and being eaten by cannibals, these are mere bagatelles as compared with the violation of the self's core." In no uncertain terms, Winnicott sets the stage for what he calls a *true self*, which is never to be communicated, as it ought to remain a pure potentiality, inexhaustible by any actuality: "We must feel able to shut out the external world and maintain our right to an inviolable privacy within ourselves." One surprising example of this act of resistance is Freud's suspicious disregard for the infantile stage, and its link to his own self-analysis. Sigmund was his mother's eldest. Amalia used to call him "my golden Sigi," while he consistently maintained a positive view of her. No wonder that in one of his introductory lectures he calls the mother-son dyad "the most free from ambivalence of all human relationships." But when Sigi was eleven months old, his narcissistic bliss was shattered: a brother was born, and the golden boy got jealous. Eight months later, baby Julius died. The mourning mother withdrew and became even less available, compensating for the loss of her second son by having six more children over the course of eight years. Yet the father of psychoanalysis barely faced his repressed anger toward his idealized mother, who first held him so tight, and then let him slip.

45.　　Now I finally see how Fairbairn's moral defense is unwittingly used by Freud (following squarely in the footsteps of Augustine, Hobbes, and Nietzsche) to tell his edifying tale about our civilization and its discontents. Looking at humanity through a series of well-aligned theological, political, moral, and psychological lenses led the West to the conclusion that its troubles come from the possession of mighty animalistic instincts that can be civilized only up to a point. For Guntrip, this turns out to be our greatest self-deception. We have "preferred to boost our egos by the belief that even if we are bad, we are at any rate strong." In so doing we have "resisted recognition of the truth that we distort our instincts into antisocial drives in our struggle to suppress the fact that deep within our make-up we retain a weak, fear-ridden infantile ego that we never completely outgrow." In short, we would rather pretend that we are bad than admit that we are weak. Yet to blame this original frailty on the parents is a diversion tactic. Human beings come from weakness and return to weakness, from infancy to senility, from insecurity to helplessness. The power one wills in between is the exception to a fragile and frightened existence that is life's basic rule.

46.   Being bad, not controlling the inner beast, resisting the process of socialization: in Guntrip's final analysis, these rationalizations of sexual or aggressive conflicts are essentially "defenses against withdrawal, regression, and depersonalization." We use them because we fail to face "the terrors of realizing how radically small, weak and cut off, shut in and unreal" we ultimately are. Human beings are violable long before they are violent. Eros and Thanatos are both sucked back into the dark void of primal Chaos from which they came. Hence the most elementary problem imaginable is this schizoid position of "feeling a nobody, of never having grown an adequate feeling of a real self." To be able to truly acknowledge our fundamental weakness is not only meant to bring about a shift in the center of gravity within psychoanalytic theory, but to lead to a "radical reassessment of all philosophical, moral, educational, and religious views of human nature." This is not to suggest that no thinker ever considered life's weakness to be the very foundation of the world. Pascal, for one, claims that nothing is more certain than the fact that people were, are, and will be weak: "What amazes me most is to see that everyone is not amazed at his own weakness."

47.   What if Freud decided to use a Jewish myth about a wandering father fully prepared to sacrifice his own son, instead of a Greek myth about a son unknowingly killing his sovereign father? And what if Freud further focused his analytic attention on Isaac's disorienting sense of being forsaken, rather than on Abraham's unwavering grip of faith? It would have led more people to recognize that the suppression of aggression is nothing in comparison to the suppression of love. It would have facilitated a clearer shift of focus from narcissists investing their libidinal energy in their oversized egos to schizoids who cannot help but persecute their frail selves. And it would have brought about a better understanding of the contempt and scorn displayed by many toward their own need to depend on other people, which Guntrip associates with the pervasive "fear and hate of weakness that is embedded in our cultural attitude." My personal blindness to all that allowed me to spend the first half of my protected life in a rural municipality in Israel called *Misgav*, which means *fortress*, *shelter*, or *haven*, as the next two decades on the island of Manhattan calmly proceeded with my being convinced of my own power to take control of my entire life. But then the idea for this notebook began to hatch.

48.   Last year was rough: for the first time in our lives, Netta and I both underwent surgeries, first to remove a tissue from her right breast, then to repair a tear in my right shoulder. The procedures went well and we fully recovered. But something in me softened. Doing my best to hold on to Netta when the ground fell out from beneath her feet, and then relying on her compassionate care while I was debilitated, turned these sudden blows into simple lessons in codependency. Facing my physical and emotional vulnerabilities in the opioid haze of sleepless convalescence, I was simultaneously regressing into a young boy and progressing into an old man. I began to think of myself less as an agent who acts in the world and more as a patient who is acted upon. In my lucky case, though, suffering at the hands of an external other or an external force is the least of my worries. My struggle, for what it is worth, has always been an inner one, though I have failed to admit it, until now. Fairbairn and Guntrip call the unconscious force that oppresses the psyche's weaker element the *internal saboteur* or *antilibinial ego*, which awoke one day last summer in rural Maine, as I suddenly slipped while climbing up a waterfall and dislocated my shoulder.

49.   Resenting, obstructing, abusing, or outright torturing the soul's derelict core—this sadomasochistic deadlock is not confined to the micro-level of an individual's inner workings. On the macro-level, I can imagine the same insidious dynamic at play in a turn against the vulnerable origins of our species. Was the prehistoric homo sapiens really noble and mighty, or was it usually just frightened, given its fragile position nowhere near the top of the food chain? I don't think that society is sapping our strong natural instincts, as Nietzsche would have it, but simply hiding how delicate we all still are. A wild animal is more likely to be helpless than fearless. Hence my hypothesis: racist hate is directed at whoever happens to represent this primordial peril stemming from the collective infancy of the human race, which the Western imagination usually projects onto an African savannah or the Middle East (the *cradle* of civilization). The bodies of those who are superstitiously and wrongly believed to be tethered to these mythological regions of bare lives — people of color, Black people, Semitic people — are violated or excluded in a symbolic ceremony that purges not sin but the inherent weakness of the human race, which neither the blindness of racism nor the progress of civilization can ever eliminate.

50.   Once upon a time a child pointed at Fanon and said: *Mama, see the Negro! I'm frightened!* According to Fanon, the child was scared *of* him, but could they be scared *for* him? Is a Black body *phobogenic* since it induces the fear that it will harm me, or that I, being white, will harm it? *Look, he's like me, a little kid who always needs their Mommy*. Ultimately everybody is a crybaby. The bullies who prey on kids at school are no exception but the rule, dramatized each recess: their external will to power is a cover-up for an even stronger inner will to weakness. It is not a triumph of the self but a sad sign of its impending collapse. Though I was not a physically violent teenager, I have verbally made the lives of classmates on whom I smelled weakness more difficult than they already were, even Netta's. But ever since we got together, as the schizoid force gradually overtook my mental apparatus, the popular kid with the sharp tongue faded into a lonesome adult scribbling in notebooks. As new relationships rarely materialized, my remaining self-confidence masked the ironic fact that, in all the circles to which I belonged since high school, my social status has been comparable to that of the childhood friends I used to put down. A big tree seems to harm no one, and a mature schizoid deep in his isolated hole tends to be treelike.

51.   No schizoid worthy of this name can naturally lead a movement or direct an institution. Schizoids are more or less inoculated against the sovereign bug. But are these antisocial tendencies abnormal, considering that humans are political animals, at least according to Aristotle? Can *schizoid politics* be more than an oxymoron? Arendt argues that totalitarianism is made possible by "the fact that loneliness, once a borderline experience usually suffered in certain marginal social conditions like old age, has become the everyday experience of the ever-growing masses of our century." Seventy years later, her insight is truer than ever. Rather than coming together to converse in the public sphere, growing apart is the order of the day. It appears, then, that a schizoid specter is ghosting the globe. I am surely in no position to criticize the modern alienation of atomized citizens, catalogue the dangers of isolation, and appeal for a reclamation of communal solidarity. The point of no return is long past, like it or not. Losing hope in meaningful relations and mutual recognition is not only the end of traditional politics, but also the start of a new thought that might encapsulate a very different kind of hope, which is partly inspired by the old practice of monastic life.

52.   What I have in mind is beautifully illustrated in a story about St. Francis, who wondered, *what is perfect joy?* Even if the masters of theology in Paris entered his Order, along with the archbishops and kings beyond the Alps, he reasoned, this would still not be true joy. Even if his friars converted the unbelievers, while he was given the power to heal the infirm and work miracles, in all these things he knew that there was no true joy. So what is true joy? In the midst of a freezing winter night, Francis returned from Perugia with muddy clothes and bleeding shins, injured by the icicles dangling from the edge of his tunic. After knocking repeatedly on his monastery's gate, a guard approached and asked for his name, so he simply replied that he was Francis. "Go away," said the incredulous guard, "it is not a decent hour for traveling; you shall not enter." Francis appealed to him again, but the guard did not budge: "You are a simpleton and an idiot; you do not measure up to us." As a last resort Francis pleaded for just a temporary shelter from the cold, but the guard who still failed to recognize him said that a nearby hospital might be his best bet. Only by enduring all this patiently and without dismay, Francis finally found "perfect joy, true virtue, and the salvation of the soul."

53.   This Franciscan tale about the joy of non-recognition, reminiscent of Kafka's "Before the Law," can be updated and restated as a rather disturbing prayer: *May I be denied entrance to my own country, home, or office. May I be locked out of my phone, email, or social media. May I be canceled.* For many, this is the stuff nightmares are made of. For schizoids, especially those who hold on to even a modicum of privilege, it is a secret blessing. They understand that, rather than fight for the inclusion of others, the truly radical and exemplary political position today is to *exclude thyself*. Whereof one is in power, thereof one must remain silent, to let others speak. Listening might be my only honest option as a white man and a tenured professor. Anything else would merely be a symbolic gesture, which is what "inclusivity" at my liberal arts college usually amounts to. Autoexclusion or self-banishment is a personal responsibility that uses a sentence from Whitman's "Song of Myself" as its mantra: "I do not give lectures or a little charity, when I give I give myself." Cancel culture is effective when it comes to well-connected individuals who thrive in the public realm; for a schizoid scholar it is benign. For the disengaged and withdrawn, deplatforming oneself is wish fulfillment.

54.   Li: "My refusal to be defined by the will of others is my one and only political statement." I don't think of the term "schizoid" as a personality disorder, a disability, or an essential nature. I use it as a theoretical marker that informs a widespread way of living that intersects with the standard fare of social identities. Neither psychology nor psychiatry can claim to contain this pervasive experience. Raising schizoid consciousness and fostering schizoid critique would give a voice to a strange collective of silent participants, whose foundation lies in the swampy ground of humanity's ontological insecurity. There is no alternative, firmer land on which to build a structure that fits our present existence, and the swamp cannot be drained. Trying to eliminate the uncertainty surrounding our very being is rather hopeless, though any sustained attempt to face it, such as Heidegger's ontology, is an endeavor I personally cannot help but respect. Granted, it is Fairbairn and Guntrip who managed to narrate the schizoid's journey through this precarious life. Yet to imagine the coming schizoid politics, it is not enough to co-opt Agamben's work for my own purposes. It also requires an appreciation of the anti-social turn in Queer and Black Studies, which keeps a wary eye on optimistic communitarian gestures of recognition and redress, reconciliation and redemption.

55.   Agamben's political thought, like Kafka's fictional work, is not interested in the ways law applies to life. The big question is: how does the law *abandon* a life. But as Nancy taught Agamben, "love alone can abandon." He elaborates: "it is by the possibility of abandonment that one knows the possibility, inverted or lost, of love." Banishment is not indifference; quite the opposite. Even though our political space pretends to be a benevolent holding environment, as Winnicott would call it, Agamben rightly suspects that every relationship harbors a potential abandonment and the threat of exclusion. This view makes him throw the baby out with the bathwater, as he imagines a new politics "set free from every figure of relation." There is, however, one telling exception. Following Foucault, he rejects the idea of a subject as an author or sovereign who relates to an external object. There is, in fact, no subject but only *subjectification*, a process of transforming oneself by *relating* to oneself. The subject is therefore nothing but this relationship. Agambenian politics is not about the relation to a law or a norm, but about the relation of the self to itself. Still, what about relating to others? And what about the schizoid self who prefers to abandon itself?

56.   A political life that revolves around the struggle for recognition by private individuals or social identities is nothing more than the continuation of war by other means. The game remains the same, albeit with slightly different players, motivated by a hope that the rules might eventually also change. In the meantime, the diversity of bodies, occupying an identical arrangement of a very limited number of seats, reaches an agreement, motivated by either fear or benefit, to accept the present order, rather than upend it. The reigning dialectics of privileged inclusion and disowned exclusion barely budges. Schizoids, however, rarely give or receive recognition; they are indifferent to both. Instead, they often engage in what today is called *ghosting.* To ghost someone is not to convey that they are nothing to you (as is usually assumed, out of insecurity); it is to say, without words, that you are nothing to them. Ghosting is silently stating that whatever relation we previously had makes no sense anymore, so it must be buried without explanation, which the dead cannot provide. If there is anything left to be recognized, it is precisely that we are ghosts, which can be difficult to digest. There is nothing more desperate than a ghost who has yet to realize that it is already dead.

57.   A person trapped in a threatening situation that is physically inescapable, like a prisoner in a concentration camp, can temporarily *dissociate* her self from the world. Since the camp offered no exit other than death, Laing observes that "the only way out was by a psychical withdrawal 'into' one's self and 'out of' the body." Even in less extreme experiences, dissociation is expressed by saying things like: *This seems unreal; I can't believe this is true; It is not happening to me.* For those whose existence is anyhow split, the entire external reality can appear to be constantly closing in on them. Such people see the world as "a prison without bars, a concentration camp without barbed wire." So while "the paranoiac has specific persecutors," the schizoid feels "*persecuted by reality itself.* The world as it is, and other people as they are, are the dangers." In my mind, dissociation is a revolt against a world that promises to be a space for politics but rarely delivers on that promise. It is not a psychological bug but a radical ethical feature, producing a detached, spectral subject who is "precluded from a full experience of realness and aliveness," for whom sustaining a creative relation with an other reaches an impasse of "a quasi it-it interaction instead of an I-thou relationship."

58.   What does a schizoid want? Ideally the answer is *nothing*. Behind some superficial desires hides a deeper desire to have no desires whatsoever. It is nearly impossible to come across a complete schizoid in real life, whose will is absolutely nowhere to be found. However a limit-case does exist: the figure of the *muselmann*, a type of concentration camp inmate who was so exhausted, physically and mentally, that he neither resisted when the guards beat him up, nor did he reach for food when some was offered. But the Nazis' nihilistic project did not stop with the production of these bare lives, stripped of their political form, dissociated from humanity. My sister once said that Hitler clearly won by instilling in the minds of the survivors and their descendants, our family included, this gnawing sense of nothingness. It made me think of how Israel is constituted by this destitution, by doing everything so the Jewish people will "never again" be nothing, above all by bullying and erasing the Palestinian people. So what is really fueling this historically deep and infinitely complex regional conflict: mutual hatred or a shared ontological insecurity? Anger or hunger? But is there anything special about this case? Can any modern state ever rise above what Klein calls its paranoid-schizoid position?

59.   Social distancing is a schizoid dream come true. Alone together, everybody is experiencing under quarantine what certified schizoids have been feeling all along. It can be heard in the voice of those for whom this newfound cocooning becomes a validation of a secret truth. It can be gleaned from the uncertainty of whether you need protection from others, or others need protection from you. Either way, the anxiety that *our love can destroy the ones we love* reigns supreme. Some say that we weren't ready for this pandemic, but I think that we were actually pretty well prepared, at least given the cornucopia of digital tools developed in the past decades to perfectly cater to the present shut-in moment. The toll of this separation can go unnoticed by those who can afford to stay indoors and online, until a bike ride through Manhattan's desolate streets laid bare the empty shell where I once perceived the city's "landscape built of sheer life." When every interpersonal connection is presented as a possible contagion, it seems that the only responsible civic engagement is to call off "all political activities and all social relations" until further notice. But while Agamben is sounding this general alarm, I'm wondering in particular where the schizoid genie will lead us once it is out of its isolated bottle.

60.   The schizoid logic works like a *pharmakon*, a drug that can either debilitate the body politic or fortify it in unforeseen ways. By testing its different effects on my own life over the years, for better or for worse, this notebook is really a logbook of my self-experimentation, which might be of value for some future study of the schizoid society that we currently live in. To this end, it would be worthwhile to finally address a common confusion, using the limited tools at my disposal. I see schizophrenia as an acute manifestation of a breakdown of the general schizoid position and its various strategies. While the two exist on a single spectrum, schizophrenia is the limit case of the schizoid configuration. For my purposes, the schizoid is a functioning schizophrenic. Schizoids hold themselves together by employing a variety of defense mechanisms — their symptoms — as they struggle to partake in everyday life and maintain what they have, who they are, and, most important, *that* they are, without breaking apart to expose their fragile, fragmented, nihilistic, and catatonic self, which is kept locked, as it were, in a safe. Does this begin to explain why schizophrenia has received such disproportionate cultural attention, while the schizoid position remains largely unknown?

61.   Deriving the schizoid from the schizophrenic is like trying to understand nuclear power by exclusively focusing on meltdowns. Nietzsche said that he is not a man, that he is dynamite. But I'm not exploding. I'm imploding, like a detonating bomb watched in reverse. In an explosion, an overfull body must extend beyond itself in a kind of ecstasy. Implosion, or *instasy*, occurs when the body seems like a void, as external objects rush in to fill it from the outside, from the surface to the empty core. Everything is collapsing inward to enter this black hole of the soul. Inspired by Deleuze and Guattari's approach to schizophrenia, I also consider the schizoid that I am as a "conceptual persona who lives intensely within the thinker and forces him to think," rather than as a pathology that "represses the living being and robs him of his thought." Can schizoid tactics transform from clinical symptoms to lines of flight? It is clear by now that my goal is not to block the schizoid experience but to put it to new use. Here, however, is where the comparison to *Anti-Oedipus* ends. Looking at the West's capitalist society, I detect schizoid configurations that overshadow the schizophrenic ones. Deleuze and Guattari's schizoanalysis only scraped the mad and melting tip of this submerged iceberg.

62.   There is an old tendency in the artistic and intellectual avant-garde to depict schizophrenia in redeeming terms: as liberation from the symbolic order or the constraint of normalcy, as an embrace of an unalienated reality or unrepressed desire, as the id incarnate. A person with schizophrenia becomes a Dionysian hero of unfettered creativity, subverting rational thought, common sense, and civilized behavior. Sass debunks this tradition by pointing out that most schizophrenics, like many schizoids, show "not an overwhelming by but detachment from the instinctual sources of vitality, not immersion in the sensory surround but disengagement from a derealized external world." At times a surfeit of consciousness or hyperawareness can turn the inner world into "a place not of darkness but of relentless light." As reason and introspection go into overdrive, the body's instincts are dimmed and affects are flattened. In these and other ways schizophrenics engage in the *unworlding* of their world, leading to an unresponsive or uncommunicative death-in-life. If they still have an ability or willingness to talk, their confused speech is not an expression of pent-up impulses, but a sign of a severe incapacity to relate to other people, whose mere touch and even gaze are perceived as threats.

63.   Other than widespread loneliness, the schizoid form of life can easily go unnoticed. Most schizoids pass as vaguely normal, both to themselves and to others. Sometimes they can even be considered successful by common standards, especially within the context of modern life (Sass and McWilliams associate the disorder with an impressive list of creative luminaries). By contrast, the rare events of schizophrenic madness are promptly flagged as exceptions that require isolation from regular society. So while the great drama of schizophrenia remains a well-contained object of endless curiosity, the largely asymptomatic schizoid tendency continues to spread inconspicuously, reproducing itself across centuries and continents. But I don't want to give the wrong impression that a schizoid existence is a stroll in the park, or a badge of honor, particularly for artists and authors, but also mathematicians and coders, or anyone whose work is done in isolation. By and large, it is a one-way path not to the celebration of genius but to a life of irrelevance. How far can one go without knowing how to relate to others, how to "network"? After more than twenty years living in such a well-connected metropolis, I feel like the very same nobody I was when I arrived.

64.   The schizoid motto is not *divide and conquer* but *divide or breakdown*. If schizophrenia is the lurking danger, then division is the first line of defense. As a response to strain, these splits may not kill you, though they will probably make you weaker. All the neat conceptual dualisms schizoids have introduced into this world may be artificial, simplistic, or just false. But the alternative is too often neither emancipatory nor practical, as it can lead to personal fragmentation and interpersonal paralysis. Questioning or playing with some distinctions, rewriting the ruts of our existence, is occasionally necessary. But unplugging the dualism machine is virtually impossible, if only because the structure it produces is part and parcel of our form of life. Philosophers can be divided into those who assert separations to fight schizophrenic atrophy, and those who undermine them to resist the schizoid tyranny. I usually belong to the first group, as the previous sentence demonstrates. Those who belong to the second tend to do so by appealing to a monistic unity (as Spinoza did), or by embracing a pluralistic multiplicity (as Deleuze did). Both groups fit Wittgenstein's observation that "philosophy is a tool which is useful only against philosophers and against the philosopher in us."

65.   The dissolution of the self can look like a scary problem, but it might also be the whole point. According to Hoffmann, my first great teacher and mentor, Buddhist thought doesn't protect from ontological insecurity but *promotes* it. He uses Laing's term to draw a striking comparison between psychotic experiences and meditation practices, wondering whether the schizoid's great fear is what a major strand in Eastern philosophy sees as pure liberation. In Mahayana Buddhism, Nirvana is the ability to let go of the most basic division of subject and object once its illusory nature is fully embraced. Nirvana does not stand in opposition to Samsara, the painful cycle of mundane existence, but lies in the *convergence* of these two notions in an enlightened insight. Hoffmann explains that "according to the Mahayanic view of the unity of Samsara and Nirvana, suffering originates not in existence itself, but in the *wrong view* of existence: it is the common categorization of the world into subject and object, I and other, which brings about human suffering." In other words, if I were to deactivate the tired separation between the world and my life, if the two somehow became one, then I could finally be released from the urge to either negate the external world or escape from it.

66.   We are skeptical of Freud's induction of a universal human psyche from his analysis of a few "hysterical" Viennese women. But how close are we to a more culturally specific understanding of our mental makeup? Devereux starts with the idea that "each ethnic group has its own typical and privileged neurosis or psychosis," and ends with a sweeping diagnosis of the "ethnic personality of modern man" as "basically schizoid," perpetually inclined to an "asocial turning inward." Occidental humanity is "*taught* to be schizoid outside the psychiatric hospital and therefore to be schizophrenic within it." Much of Western culture champions individuals who are aloof, not displaying affect, giving no warmth, and declining emotional involvement with others. Observing people on the streets in European and American cities, Devereux detected "a disconcerting smell of the back wards of a mental hospital harboring burnt-out schizophrenics." Another clear manifestation of our schizoid society: disaffected sex is *de rigueur*. People learn how to disguise under various pretenses the "incapacity to love and *to make love* (as distinct from fornicating)." If only these insights from the mid-twentieth century took into account online hookup culture. Also, since when did texting make calling feel so wrong?

67.　　Can capital care, feel, or love? When relationships are primarily transactional, no wonder people prefer self-checkout lanes as they listen to their noise-canceling headphones. It is almost too easy to take such cliché descriptions of the alienated capitalist, which are as old as the young Marx, and apply them to the schizoid. What is slightly less obvious is what I would like to call *collective schizo-capitalism*: gated communities, private schools, corporate culture, luxury leisure, or whatever else is included in what Sloterdijk calls the Crystal Palace. Economic privilege allows some to safely relate only to those who are just like them — plus a few others whose symbolic difference is carefully curated, closely managed, and duly celebrated — while the true others are kept at a secure distance. At the same time, social media companies stopped even pretending to facilitate relations between their users, who establish instead an abusive relationship with the applications themselves. As Debord explained long ago, once capital "is accumulated to the point where it becomes image," the resulting spectacle ends up doing a clever double duty: first it separates humans from each other, and then it gives these lonely individuals an illusory sense of connectivity and unity.

68.   Rather than linking up the entire globe with a shared experience, cyberspace tends to cloister each body in a semiotic bubble. At issue is not the adverse effects of a digital apparatus on a living being, but the slightly more complicated constellation involving more than a single person plus some screens. To illustrate, Netta is on her phone, while I feel a bit neglected, so I open my laptop, not because I have something to do, but just to cope with the feeling, which she interprets as my own disconnect, so she retreats further, which makes me do the same, creating a negative feedback loop that leads to ever-greater separation. Designed by and for schizoids, humans are willing to interact with their attentive machines, be recognized by them, and put their trust in them, because they are reluctant to do so with each other. Turing asks, *am I talking to a computer?* While I ask, *am I mentally attached to it?* As long as technology exploits our disappointments and emotional vulnerabilities, it just wants to be a *symptom*: it pretends to solve our problems without really addressing them, exploiting a pathology instead of helping us face it. For example, the priority of *showing* over *giving* encourages us to exhibit ourselves online but not to get emotionally involved with others.

69.   Weil illustrates the other side of this coin: "There is no man, however hard-hearted, who does not feel compassion about the affliction presented in the theater. This is because he can be disinterested; he has nothing to gain and no fear of danger or contamination. So he can lose himself in the characters of the play. He gives free rein to his compassion, because he knows the situation is unreal. If it was real he would turn as frigid as ice." The schizoid takes the extra step to become an onlooker at her own life and the lives of her loved ones. Since this personal drama seems to be playing on a distant stage, it is too often not too exciting to watch. Even when things get fascinating they don't make much of a difference, because there is little active participation in, or real experience of, the inner and outer battlefields of everyday existence. Hence Wallace's more recent description of the loneliness of the voyeuristic television viewer sitting at home, playing a "game of appearance poker" by declining to be seen and to "bear the psychic costs of being around other humans." This comment finally leads me to wonder about the potential readers of these notes. They are no more than an abstraction, looking at me like detectives behind a one-way mirror. Will they feel for me? Does it even matter?

70.   Netta's therapist explained my condition to her by comparing it to a person driving a car against traffic while being oblivious to all the honking. But there is another explanation for my anti-social tendencies. Being white as well as male seems to be a part of my problem. "What lonely entitled men are really asking for is to be cocooned from the life experiences that give other people the skills to survive loneliness." Azaad argues that less privileged individuals are prone to develop relationships and establish trust via mutual aid support systems. Self-reliance is just a ruse stemming from a failure to acknowledge one's material, spiritual, and especially personal debts. There is a very different type of loneliness that is the lot of the marginalized, but it is easily dismissed as benign by the upper class, which only gets alarmed once its own rarefied kind begins to be bothered by a paralyzing sense of isolation, leading to today's steady stream of articles about sad and lonely men. Is this notebook falling into the same trap? While so many can only dream of being left alone, I whine about my (fortunate) solitude. What is ontological insecurity when compared, for instance, with food insecurity? Has the seed of my loneliness grown into a malignant melancholy, given the soil of structural oppression (white supremacy, the patriarchy, heteronormativity) in which it has been planted?

71.   In the midst of a plague, with a political society in shambles, witnessing upheavals left and right, facing the misery and injustice of this world, I have chosen to spend such critical moments gazing at my own navel. I even have ample time to complement my daily spiritual practice with a vigorous regimen of physical exercise as a long-distance runner, since the two ideally go hand in hand. But not everybody can afford to act like a schizoid. While we are sheltering in place, many do not feel that they can allow themselves to examine their own lives, and some of those who can prefer not to, maybe because they believe that caring about other people is more urgent than the care of the self. But like students in detention who are asked to stop and think about what they were doing, no cynicism or self-righteousness can hide the fact that this mandatory isolation remains a prime time for personal reckoning and rethinking, given that there are less distractions and no excuses. Entering this "strange experiment of global monasticism," Coccia claims that, like the religious recluse of yore, we all "retreat into our private space and spend the day murmuring secular prayers." This new normal, as fleeting as it may ultimately turn out to be, seems much less at odds with my current practice of note-taking.

72.   When the Spartan King Anaxandrides was asked why his countrymen entrusted the cultivation of their lands to slaves instead of doing it themselves, he replied: "It was by not taking care of the fields, but of ourselves, that we acquired those fields." Foucault reads this as a way of saying that real privilege does not belong to the ones who let others attend to their every need, but to those who attend to their own selves. This is the true mark of superiority in both antiquity and modernity, especially when contrasted with the necessity to attend to others by serving them, or attend to a job to make a living. I definitely feel blessed in this regard. But the laconic quote says more: the care of the self is capital investment, granting its practitioners powers that enable them to obtain even more power. To put it in a formula, M-C-M, money yields self-care that yields money. There is, however, another, more subversive and less elitist angle to approach this issue. One day, Plato passed by Diogenes while the Cynic was washing some salad greens. "If you had been nicer to our ruler," Plato sneered, "you wouldn't have to wash your own greens." Diogenes replied: "If you had acquired the habit of washing your greens, you wouldn't have to be the ruler's slave."

73.   *Wash your own greens* sounds like the motto of a disjointed artistic movement that adheres to what I call, unsurprisingly, a *schizoid aesthetics*. Compare it with relational art, which encourages intersubjective encounters between audience members, who form a contingent collective wherever and whenever the work is on display. But there is not necessarily a concrete object to behold, other than the ephemeral community created within this artificial environment (for example, Tiravanija's installation in which he cooked pad thai in a gallery space and served it to the visitors, which I enjoyed, admittedly, not because it led to interesting interactions, but because it was tasty free food). Schizoid art, by contrast, is non-relational out of defiance or indifference. Whether it is intended for the public, made public, or finds a public, is beside the point. It is self-involved and self-referential, not self-expressive. Schizoid writers love to invoke the death of the author, but if anyone is dead to them, it's the reader. The tentacles of schizoid aesthetics reach outsider art, self-published as well as posthumous works, creative practices without a finished product, and whatever is homemade or DIY. If I were Benjamin, I would speak about the work of art in the age of working on oneself.

74.   Before the twenty-first century, an *it girl* had to "go out, be seen, and be charming," letting others take her photos at all the right parties. These days, Stagg claims that fashionable girls "will most likely have been discovered by social media. Their art direction, more than anything else, gets them through doors. They are, more often than not, self-described homebodies, even antisocial. Today, a cool girl is coaxed from a bedroom iPhone shoot into a professional studio." As painful as loneliness can be, it is also pretty chic. Girlfriends or boyfriends still exist in real life, but they can be excised from these influencers' self-curated image online. Another contemporary phenomenon I am unqualified to theorize is *hikikomori*. Since the turn of the century, a growing number of Japanese men have been refusing to leave their rooms for months and even years at a stretch. Out of school and out of work, these modern hermits often have their parents take care of them well into adulthood. Their reclusiveness is speculated to be triggered by a reluctance to fit into the society that first scarred them and then shamed them for going into hiding. Even though a *hikikomori* appears to be the diametrical opposite of an *it girl*, aren't they both cut from the same schizoid cloth?

75.   Are shut-ins really alone if they participate in a multiplayer video game? To complicate the tired association of the physically isolated and digitally connected, consider the curious case of a man who "had spent nearly forty years lounging around at home, dressed in pajamas, a bathrobe, and slippers," directing from his Playboy Mansion "the largest-circulation men's magazine in the United States without leaving the house, often without leaving his bed." Hefner's round bed, which was wired to a state-of-the-art array of telecommunication devices, turned, since the 1960s, into his central office, as well as a multimedia production platform. Bedridden by choice and domesticated by predilection, he is a critical paradigm for today's shift toward work from home. His publication promoted the image of a man who does not need to sport either business suits or outdoorsy boots to prove his masculinity. Shunning traditional family roles as sons, husbands, and fathers, its readers discovered new ways to design and use their interior space, which up to then was coded feminine. The bachelor pad was a Freudian site where one could seek pleasures, not persons. As Preciado demonstrates, an Eames lounge chair and the girl next door can become nearly interchangeable objects of desire.

76.   Knausgård: "My basic feeling is that of the world disappearing, that our lives are being filled with images of the world, and that these images are inserting themselves between us and the world, making the world around us lighter and lighter and less and less binding." But words, he realized more than 3,000 pages into *My Struggle*, can have the same effect: "I had tried to involve myself in the life around me, normal life, the one everyone lived, but I'd failed, and so strong was my sense of defeat, this glimpse of shame, that little by little, unbeknown to myself as well, I shifted the focus of my life, pushed it further and further into literature in such a way that it didn't seem like a retreat, as though I were seeking a refuge, but like a strong and triumphant move, and before I knew what was happening it had become my life. [...] It wasn't because I had problems with the social world that I withdrew from, no, it was because I was a great writer or wanted to be one. That solved all my problems and I thrived on it. But if it was true that I was hiding, what was I frightened of? I was frightened of other people's judgments of me, and to avoid this I avoided them." I know exactly what he means. Our schizoid struggles align, in all their masculine, bourgeois, pathetic glory.

77.   In the land of the schizoid, the autofiction author is king, or queen. As contemporary writers grew tired of made-up characters and situations, they began mining their personal experience as prime material for a kind of prose that invades their own privacy. But there is rarely anything remarkable about these novelists' lives, other than the act of writing their surprisingly compelling stories. Personally, I still find that reading autofiction is a small act of faith in these authors, who frequently feign a lack of belief in themselves. For anyone who is not so interested in getting absorbed into pretend worlds, the allure of the novel as a beacon of empathy, or as a training session in moral imagination, also gradually fades away. As an alternative, the genre of autofiction "offers a reminder of what the world looks like without a constant awareness of the perspectives of others." For Dames, this "recovery of solitude" makes special sense in a hyper-connected society. If a book of autofiction (or autophilosophy) teaches us anything, it is *how to stay separate*. But it is less instructive when it comes to how to hold a clear mirror up to oneself. The forefather of the self-centered literary genre is a case in point: "nobody," it has been observed, "knows himself less" than Rousseau.

78.   A familiar twist in plots about deep-space explor-
ation is the hero who agonizes over an earthly human
relationship that the interstellar mission left unresolved.
Unable to live in the terrestrial here and now, or mourning
what is no longer in the here and the now, the astronaut
finds in faraway stars the ultimate escape from Mother
Earth, which apparently proved to be bad enough. Whenever I'm on vacation in Israel, where I spend many charged
hours with friends and family every day, my ordinary existence on the lonely island of Manhattan is thrown into
relief, where I am often bereft of all that, as if there is no
gravity, no oxygen, no friction, and no relation to write
home about, other than Netta. Since *A Theory of a City*, I
have sensed that New York is the schizoid capital of the
world. Much of what was achieved here in the past century
reflects this modern disorder. Its urban energy is fueled
by eight million lonely souls who treat their work as their
prime salvation. Many of those who call it home remain,
existentially speaking, homeless. New York is not a metropolis (mother city) but an *orbapolis* (orphan city), barely
able to love and hold its denizens, as its ego is split into
a tale of two cities: fantasy and reality, private and public,
shadow and sunshine.

79.   Like Nietzsche's slave revolt in morality, the schizoid revolt that has been determining the destiny of Western culture since its inception is only now coming into focus, at least wherever I look. My hunch is that homo schizoid is not an abnormality of humanity but its exemplary manifestation. The schizoid position pretends to exclude its holders from any shared experience, while in reality it guarantees their very inclusion. In a way, we are living in a schizoid world. Our world was not built by people who knew how to relate to each other, but by people who were scarred. Their scar is what propelled them into the future. Every document of civilization is a document of schizoism. To be ontologically insecure means that you can't just *be*. Instead, you must *do*, incessantly. What one does overtakes what one is, which verges on nothing. To stop producing, consuming, speaking, or scrolling is to grow naked and cold. Winnicott: "After being — doing and being done to. But first, being." Otherwise, the deeds of active persons are like the movements of a headless chicken, covering up the fact that deep down they no longer feel that they really exist. The bottom line, which is always relational, is that I *am* something for other people, before and after the things I *do* for them. Or so I hope.

80.   What does it mean to lose the sensation of being? This sixth sense or inner touch is what neurophysiologists call *proprioception*. Sacks explains that "if a man has lost a leg or an eye, he knows he has lost a leg or an eye; but if he has lost a self — himself — he cannot know it, because he is no longer there to know it." The perception of our own being is arguably the most important sensation we have, but because of its familiarity it usually escapes our attention. This was not the case with Christina, "the disembodied lady," who had to face the horror of no longer sensing her body as her own. She was not paralyzed: she relearned how to walk, but she did not sense that she was walking. This condition is not as abnormal as it sounds, since the proprioception of infants is also not yet fully developed. Nor do they have a meaningful sense of self. Christina was special in her ability to use language to share her experience, or its lack thereof, with other people. But what is a shared sensation of being, Agamben asks, if not the true meaning of friendship? Because what is a friend, Aristotle asks, if not another self? And what is this notebook, I ask, if not an exercise in proprioception? Or is this rather a testament to its colossal collapse? Can an undivided self ever know itself?

81.   While Laing solidified the reputation of the schizoid as a *divided self*, the lesser-known New York psychoanalyst Jeffrey Seinfeld (not Jerry) really hit the nail on the head by defining the schizoid as an *empty core*. The empty core is felt "as a lack disrupting the sense of boundedness or wholeness." It is not a static void, but "the hunger for objects internal and external. It is a state of insufficiency and activity through suction and pulsion." There are two strategies to handle a life that presents itself as a bottomless pit: you can either eliminate all need and treat the emptiness as an ideal, or you can reach a stage of fulfilled completion, which is also a way to extinguish need, but through satiation. This reminds me of my mom, leaning over once during lunch, whispering into my ear, "*nothing* pleases him," while smirking in the direction of my dad, who was silently concentrating on his plate. She meant that *anything* would satisfy him. But the alternative, that his happiness lies in nothingness, kept her jab stuck in my head for days. My own empty self makes it seem as if I don't deserve to possess or consume or just experience things, let alone enjoy them. Today's maxim, *treat thyself*, rarely resonates. There *is* pleasure, plenty of pleasure, just not for me.

82.   On the first day of each semester, I ask my new students to introduce themselves and answer a simple question, in any way they find fit: *Why are you here?* After we go around the room, when it is my turn, I reply by playing a short clip from Sesame Street, and claim that when I saw it on television, in first grade, the seed of my future as a philosophy professor was planted. This clip, dare I say, is my Rosebud. In it, Billy, a little furry monster, asks Grover and Herry, a couple of older monsters, to explain the difference between *here* and *there*. To this end, Herry walks away as Grover tells Billy that they are both *here* while Herry is *there*. "But I want to be *there*," Billy cries. Walking over to stand by Herry, Billy rejoices that he is now *there*, only to be corrected that he is actually *here*. Frustrated, he walks back and forth between Grover and Herry, demanding each time to be *there*, which is always where he is not, or where the other is. Then the two exasperated and rather unhelpful monsters decide to abandon Billy, yelling at him from a distance to "stay *there*." This makes the little monster very happy. He repeatedly and cheerfully declares that he is finally *there.* Until his worried mother arrives. "I've been looking all over for you," she says. "What are you doing *here*!?"

83.   While the topic of loss and lack dominates the psychoanalytic discourse, *what is missing* is open to debate. The central problem that the British tradition of object relations theory, and by extension this notebook, is set to confront, is actually that of the lost *subject* or absent self. But there is a more fashionable school of thought, developed in France during the same decades, which actually revolves around the other problem of the lost *object*. While staying loyal to the Oedipal complex and the concept of the drive, Lacan made, almost despite himself, a crucial contribution to object relations theory, to which Seminar IV is dedicated. The lecture notes insist that the true object to which a subject wishes to relate is, in some fundamental sense, always already gone. Every attempt to regain this elusive object remains insufficient. It is that which we can neither get a hold on nor let go of. It gnaws at our psyche, whether we know it, or like it, or not. Such an experience of object lack is the basic meaning of desire. Consequently, complete pleasure from sexual relations is virtually impossible. You can *never* get what you want. Good enough is not good enough. While Freud assumes that we seek pleasures, and Fairbairn thinks that we seek persons, Lacan believes that we seek phantasms.

84.   The Lacanian subject is a schizoid of sorts, recently characterized as the *one-all-alone,* whose relations to others are nothing but a growing string of frustrations. Again, Kafka's lonely protagonists exemplify this predicament: the unattainable objects—the trial, the castle, America, plus their representatives—render K. a dead man walking, for whom a sustainable loving relation with another person seems like science fiction. Lacan, however, holds that true love *requires* absence in order to thrive. A gift coming from someone who has everything is not a real sign of love. And loving someone perfect who possesses the fullness of all that can be had is equally pointless. Even in God something seems to be missing: "There is no reason to love God save that perhaps He doesn't exist." Lacan therefore argues that love is founded on a subject's acceptance of the object's lack. The subject-object relation either points to something *beyond* the relationship, or else there is a veil *between* the two (which either hides what one has, or what one doesn't have). Relations get creative and dynamic due to this unfathomable element. We rarely approach the object of desire in a straight line, and usually dance around it. This dance *is* the relationship, rather than its preamble.

85.   A striking summary of Lacan's slippery approach was made three centuries before his time by Pascal: "We are floating in a medium of vast extent, always drifting uncertainly, blown to and fro; whenever we think we have a fixed point to which we can cling and make fast, it shifts and leaves us behind; if we follow it, it eludes our grasp, slips away, and flees eternally before us. Nothing stands still for us. This is our natural state and yet the state most contrary to our inclinations. We burn with desire to find a firm footing, an ultimate, lasting base on which to build a tower rising up to infinity, but our whole foundation cracks and the earth opens up into the depth of the abyss." Today more than ever, we are drowning in signs and symbols, images and fantasies, a proliferation of endless digital objects to which we try to relate, even though they can feel partial, unreal, fleeting, distorted, or promiscuous. How hard it is to just stay with the feeling, live with the discomfort, dwell on the thought, hold on to the person, for the long run. "If there is one thing that lies at the base and the foundation of all analytic experience," Lacan mused, "it's that we find it so very hard to apprehend what is most real around us, that is to say, human beings such as they are."

86.   The books I wrote are no substitutions for the people to which I have failed to relate. By now at least I know that nothing can fill this interpersonal hole. Thanks to Lacan, I also no longer assume that "everything is resolved when the subject's relations with his fellow man are, as they say, person-to-person relations and not relations with an object." Referring to the lives I care about in my life as objects is, of course, not an attempt to degrade them into dumb things — to *objectify* — but actually a way to place them center stage. The insular subject only begins to make sense once relationships with significant objects within its circle gain some clarity. This is the legacy of what I call Object-Relations Ontology. An object is not whatever is in my purview, but only what I *cathect* with, what I am emotionally invested in. What a subject is completely indifferent towards is never an object. Both subject and object are simply conceptual positions humans take when they relate to each other, and they flip according to one's perspective (from yours, I am an object; from mine, you are). In this technical sense, the idea of intersubjectivity, of a relation between two subjects, is a contradiction in terms. An intersubjective relation is like a shoe that fits another shoe rather than a foot.

87.   Instead of treating an object as a subject, what if I could stop *relating* to objects and start *using* them? Winnicott's use of the word *use* can be frustrating. Like *object*, the psychoanalytic meaning gets confused with its everyday implication: to use persons is not to take advantage of them, but to approach them as real and independent, rather than as extensions of my imagination. When we first relate to new people, we project onto them our pre-existing notions and feelings. Winnicott suggests that two things need to happen before another being can be seen for what it is and not for what you want it to be: the relationship experiences a rift, which then gets mended. An object becomes useful if it is still there after it was almost lost. For example, the first year I saw my therapist, he seemed more like an internal fantasy than an external person. After my frustration with the treatment led to its termination, I came across a description of the schizoid position and began to study it on my own. My self-diagnosis led me back to Peter with anger at his hands-off approach, starting a second year of sessions that became much more fruitful. Translation: "The subject can now *use* the object that has survived" the attempt to destroy it, while "the object develops its own autonomy and life."

88.   I am not alone in being driven by absence more than by presence. Our entire virtual culture is fueled by this predilection. Curiously, objects can feel present while absent, or absent while present. This might be the most reasonable way to answer the question, *is the object real?* Winnicott calls such objects *transitional*, as they occupy the threshold between inner and outer, individual and society, potential and actual, subjective and objective. He says that the best way to handle these objects is by *playing* with them. This recommendation is not limited to children, since transitional objects also mark the location of our whole cultural experience as adults. "Mr. Winnicott is not wrong," Lacan uncharacteristically concurs, "life is situated in the midst of all this." Lacan's example is religion and philosophy, two domains filled with notions that may only claim for themselves a kind of *demi-existence*. As I wrote on this notebook's first page, "a philosophy of myself, like every philosophy, cannot be dedicated to either private or public events, just as it cannot be labeled either fact or fiction." However, to treat the present text as a playful transitional object between the world and me is not to imply personal progress, but to seek a temporary antidote to my emotional evacuation.

89.   It is quite possible that the reason humans are less hardwired to their biological destiny than other mammals is that they require more time to develop from infancy to adulthood, and depend on more caregiving to reach this goal. It is precisely the most helpless, vulnerable, but also malleable newborns in their animal class, unprepared to face the world on their own, who slowly mature into the most creative species, dominating nature by means of their nurture. How to be a good-enough mother to these fragile yet plastic creatures was Winnicott's lifelong project (he never had kids of his own), though the practically inevitable failing of the parental instinct remains inherent to the high drama of these civilized beasts. As we grow up to navigate the cultural landscape of transitional objects (like language and art), some of us "may be leading satisfactory lives and may do work that is even of exceptional value and yet may be schizoid or schizophrenic" due to our weak sense of reality; while others may be "so firmly anchored in objectively perceived reality that they are ill in the opposite direction of being out of touch with the subjective world and with the creative approach to fact." To be somewhere in between is a Winnicottian indicator of mental health.

90.   Rather than pursuing this delicate balancing act between a true self and an external reality, resulting in an intermediate space of creative play, Lacan emphasizes another fundamental tension, in which the subject navigates between symbolic objects and real ones. "You ask for a book in a library and you're told that it's missing from its place. It might be just alongside, but it is no less the case that it's missing from its place. It is, in principle, invisible. This means that the librarian lives entirely in a symbolic world." However, what is real cannot be shaken off; it is the rock on which all fantasies ultimately crash, or the stone that always sticks to the "soles of its shoes." We rarely break through the thick crust of the symbolic order to reach the unstable and unnamable state of things, before they get captured by words and rules, traditions and institutions. And yet the lost object we strive for is not exactly real. The lack in question is once again symbolic, as in the missing library book, or in feeling castrated, given that the phallus is a signifier, not the male organ. For example, within the academy, I am an associate professor of philosophy. But then a symbolic castration makes me anxiously wonder: am I a *real* philosopher, or is it just an empty title?

91.   Despite their differences, Winnicott and Lacan both insist on the primacy of others in the formation of the self. As reasonable as this idea sounds, it reopened an old wound in the annals of psychoanalysis. At first, Freud assumed that sexual abuse in early childhood led to hysteric and neurotic adults. But in 1897 he began to entertain the possibility that his patients' molestation stories didn't really happen; that these were mostly fantasies. The fact that he sometimes stopped believing survivors of abuse was only one major problem. The other problem was that he started seeing infantile sexuality as innate, developing independently of the child's surrounding reality. As Ptolemy wanted to ensure that the earth is at the center of the universe, Freud tried to recenter an unmoved and solipsistic subject, who came into the world naturally endowed with drives. Retracing this decisive turn of events, Laplanche argues that even a normal nursing relation between an infant and a caring adult, which is in no way perverse, can still include integral elements of healthy seduction that may induce one's personal and sexual trajectory. And with this last intervention, the Copernican revolution of object relations, which took upon itself the decentering of the self, reached its logical conclusion.

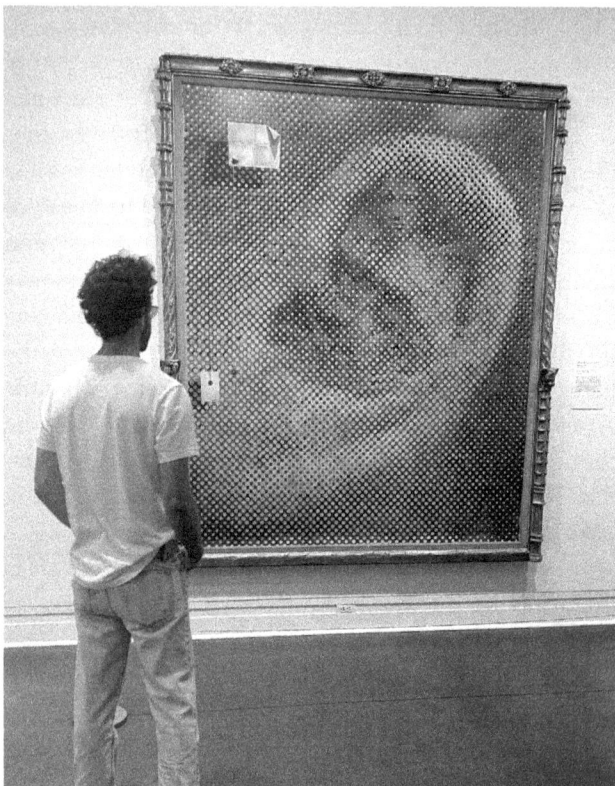

Figure 3.

92.   I was eighteen when I first set foot outside my motherland. Those few weeks in New York were decisive for my future self, in particular that morning at the Metropolitan Museum, descending a staircase while inspecting Dalí's *Madonna* from 1958. From afar, it looked like a closeup of an ear. At mid-distance, an image of a mother holding her child materialized in the ear's inner contours. As I reached the landing, the picture became an abstract collection of colorful dots. Turning the corner, a new feeling presented itself: *Netta. I think I love her.* Shortly after my return to Israel we went together to a Björk concert in the ruins of a Roman amphitheater. On the way back home I felt compelled to confess my love while we were making out on the hood of my dad's car. I'm writing this account a quarter century later, while she is working in the other room of our apartment on the Lower East Side. But that painting remains a mystery. Was I hypnotized or seduced by the resting pendulum that Dalí added at the left end of the canvas, whose weight is actually a cherry? Did a secret vestibular system in the giant ear fixed to the wall disorient the approaching viewer and catch him off balance? Is the Virgin Mary my mother or spouse? Is the baby Jesus me or our potential progeny?

93.   We were just kids when we fell in love, and we were friends for years prior. Today we are holding on to each other partly as a way to hold onto our childhood, acting as each other's relic of a pre-adult self. Somehow I knew back then that this relationship was to last for good. What I'm only realizing now is that what keeps it going is not only the way I see her and the way she sees me, but also the way I see her seeing me, and the way she sees me seeing her. Laing elaborates: "Narcissus fell in love with his image, taking it to be another. Jack falls in love with Jill's image of Jack, taking it to be himself. She must not die, because then he would lose himself. He is jealous in case any one else's image is reflected in her mirror." Hence the perfect love song would be Velvet Underground's "I'll Be Your Mirror." Still, if you could keep only one thing — either your love towards the other or the other's love towards you — which would it be? When I first came up with this thought experiment before falling asleep not long ago, both Netta and I chose the former, non-narcissistic option: we would sadly let go of the other's love to maintain our own daily expression of it. But trying to separate loving and being loved is a Solomonic split. Surely, real love is only alive when both are at play.

94.   Baldwin: "I have always felt that a human being could only be saved by another human being. I am aware that we do not save each other very often. But I am also aware that we save each other some of the time." Nothing could be closer to the truth, apart from the fixation on salvation, which upholds the very Christian tradition that his statement wishes to upend. To circumvent these theological walls, this wise American can enter a dialogue with his Greek counterpart. In a moment of great clarity, Socrates realizes that just as one is able to know oneself, an eye is able to see itself. So if he understood what it could possibly mean to say to an eye, *see thyself*, he could finally make sense of what is at stake in telling a human being, *know thyself*. Yet for an eye to truly see itself, a mirror is not good enough. Instead, the philosopher suggests looking closely into *another eye*, where a miniature image of the spectator is reflected in its dark center. Thus I can see myself in Netta's pupil, which is the exact part of her body *that can see me*. So it follows that if there is something in another human that can know you, then searching for it, and contemplating it, will lead you to know yourself. What you will then know is the part in yourself that can know an other.

95.   More than two-thirds of this notebook are finished, and I am finally coming around to saying something that is embarrassingly obvious. There is only one effective therapy that can soften, though not cure, the schizoid position. It is simply called love. Maybe any love will do, but at present I'm particularly interested in the kind of nearly mystical connection I have with Netta, which feels less like a contingent choice than a fundamental fate. It is as if my being — with none of its masks and all of its insecurities — melts into hers. Yet Guntrip has already shown that telling a schizoid, *love is all you need*, is like telling an anorexic, *food is all you need*. It is a case of cruel pessimism: the foundation of your flourishing is the very thing from which you recoil. In my case, while I am lucky to be nourished by a long-term relationship, it can also become so overwhelming that I'm left with very little space to relate to anyone else in this world. Sometimes I even think that I love Netta as much as Augustine loved God: "The soul defiles itself with unchaste love when it turns away from you and looks elsewhere for things which it cannot find pure and unsullied except by returning to you." But what kind of love precludes the possibility of loving anything other than one ultimate object?

96.   In my book on Genesis I say that the main contention of the parable of the flood is not that there is only one God, but that there is only one human. From this divine perspective, the whole world can perish as long as Noah (and company) is saved. Biblically, whenever love becomes too exclusive, no matter who is involved, catastrophe is afoot. Personally, I don't argue with Augustine calling God "the life of my life," but I do believe that corporeal relations can achieve a similar existential effect. His schizoid position stipulates that to embrace divinity is to reject reality. It is only thanks to Spinoza that we no longer feel obligated to choose between loving God and loving nature. Which raises an odd question: where am I when I love? In some heavenly city, a terrestrial city, or the point of their convergence? In *Love and Saint Augustine*, Arendt settles elsewhere: "Since the ultimate goal of the lover is his own happiness, he actually is guided in all his desires by a desire for his own good, that is, for something that is inside himself." Otherwise, "desiring and depending on things outside myself, that is, on the very things I am not," would lead to a self in a state of *dispersion* who has lost "the unity that holds me together by virtue of which I can say *I am*."

97.   If only a God can save us, then only Netta can embrace me. Initially, these totalizing holding environments
radiate safety and warmth. Eventually, a devotee can easily
be *devoured* by them, since any stab at gaining autonomy
results in feeling empty and lost. In another one of his mental *knots*, as he calls them, Laing breaks down this problem
into four stages, which correspond to my four decades on
earth: "Once upon a time, when Jack was little, he wanted
to be with his mummy all the time, and was frightened
she would go away. Later, when he was a little bigger, he
wanted to be away from his mummy, and was frightened
that she wanted him to be with her all the time. When he
grew up, he fell in love with Jill, and he wanted to be with
her all the time, and was frightened she would go away.
When he was a little older, he did not want to be with Jill
all the time, he was frightened that she wanted to be with
him all the time, and that she was frightened that he did
not want to be with her all the time." It is about time to
call a spade a spade. During my thirties, I dispersed myself
into numerous bedrooms around New York, Berlin, and
Boston, without ever getting seriously involved with any
of the strangers I slept with, but also without ever satiating
my hunger, or easing the loneliness.

98.   If Freud would call my casual encounters *displacement activities*, Fairbairn would see them as a *substitution of bodily for emotional contacts*. I never sought persons, only pleasures, which I wanted to give, more than receive. Instead of feeling anything, I wanted to make someone, anyone, feel something. Attachment, though, was anathema. The point was to become nothing more, but also nothing less, than an object, at least for an hour, before returning home, untempted by yet another siren, and restarting the Sisyphean search for a new random partner. A quote from Nelson, which she repurposed from Wittgenstein's definition of philosophy, became my guide: "Fucking leaves everything as it is. Fucking may in no way interfere with the actual use of language. For it cannot give it any foundation either. It leaves everything as it is." Meanwhile, Netta knew about my actions in general terms but without much detail. She was unaware of how extensive my sexual practice grew, as the permission I got was seldom explicit or specific. For too long, she didn't ask, and I didn't tell. In many ways, it was a situation neither of us was ready to face. Until we were forced to, one autumn day five years ago. In the wake of this crisis, from its rubble, the present notebook is still being written.

99.   An excerpt from the nonexistent Autobiography of Netta C. Yerushalmy: "I eyed him while waiting for my bag in a German airport. He had that perfect body of a veteran ballet dancer. We struck up a conversation that quickly revealed we were both in town to perform our solos in an international festival that began the next day. After the taxi ride we shared to the hotel, and a dinner with some other participants, I had no doubt where this was going. But I'd been in a committed relationship for what felt even then, a decade ago, like forever. I had had serious crushes before — the opera singer in the regional production I danced in, the set designer working on a performance with which I was involved — but this was different; this was real. When David and I had discussed this possibility in the past he was often in favor, but I was still surprised that when I called he gave me his blessing. Those sleepless nights in K's room opened a whole new chapter for me. Back in New York, it was hard to stomach that my husband had been with more than one woman already. But the freedom to do as I please, to desire and be desired, to have all the feelings — though I rarely acted upon them — led me to let his ongoing activities slide. What came next was a protracted festival of selective repression."

100.   I am grateful to all my wife's lovers. As I write this, she is in the midtown apartment of a man who has been in her life for the past year. Soon I will bike over to Williamsburg for another evening with a woman I've been seeing for months. For lack of a better term, I call these partners our *other* significant others. While Netta has never met her and I have never met him, all parties are keenly aware and warmly approve of each other. As delicate as these new and loving relations are, they also enrich our quarter-century-old core relationship. Which makes me wonder: can the line leading from the theory of object relations to the practice of open relations be both straight and queer? Can polyamory achieve the kind of social acceptance presently enjoyed by homosexuality? Like gay marriage, open marriage deserves not only legal but also cultural representation that is wider and prouder than the cringeworthy depictions available today. As things stand, it remains a marginalized form of life with which few wish to publicly identify. Serving as models for other non-monogamous couples, while disturbing the crumbling institution of marriage, sounds better than looking the other way. So why am I worried about these notes falling into the hands of a relative, or a student?

101.   The second excerpt from Netta's imaginary Auto-biography is a reproduction of an email she never sent me while on vacation: "Dear D. Every letter is a love letter. I realize that writing pains me but loving feeds me. So much of the latter is endlessly addressed to you. This muchness is real. Partly it was the hurt inflicted that made it so. I never imagined two people can revel in each other more than we do. But there is always more. You like to theorize this 'affective surplus displaced from the offspring we never pro-duced.' But I don't see it as a zero-sum game. Love is like a flame. To divide is not to take away. My feelings toward you are actually intensified by my feelings toward S. You and I are an old tree with new branches that spread out far from its ancient roots. As far away as the tropical island from which I am now writing to you. But even from here I sense your perpetual isolation. So I can only thank C, your *other* other half, for being there, with you. Soon I will return. I always do. Because I cannot really live without you, what we constantly give each other, and what you are happy to see others give me. Everybody's generosity is astounding. So I suspect that Winnicott is wrong. There's no such thing as a true self. But a true relation does exist."

102.   Doubrovsky points out that autobiography "is a privilege reserved for the important people of this world." With apologies to Stein, who ventriloquized her life partner in *The Autobiography of Alice B. Toklas*, Netta is the one who deserves to write such a book that retells the story of her genius. As for me, this minor autophilosophy will do; though I once wanted to write a book called *My Life* that is all about Netta's. I almost always miss her, even when we are in the same room. She has never left my side, yet I constantly feel deserted. But I doubt this symbiosis is only my subjective issue. Isn't she so objectively extraordinary that being in her proximity for an extended period of time can lead anyone to cancel the world that pales in comparison? If I were with someone more mundane, wouldn't I seek more external stimuli? If not all objects of desire are made equal, not all relations are as consuming as my own. Hence my limited capacity to be with others who are not her, epitomized by a scene from our wedding: this celebration of the truest relation in my life, this public acknowledgment of our private, shared existence, was too hard for me to bear. Family and friends felt like intruders, their presence pulling her away from me. So I got drunk right after the ceremony and shut myself off in a room for most of the night.

103.   In a capitalist society bent on competitive per-
fectionism, consumed by a relentless search for what is
best, Winnicott's predilection for what is *good enough* recently became a fashionable (though somewhat bastard-
ized) refrain. For example, should a self-aware writer living
through this socially conscious present be governed by a
lingering fear of causing offense or appearing oblivious, or
can I let myself come across on these pages as just a good-
enough person? Can Netta and I be no more than good-
enough for each other? As we are joining the shriveled
middle class and entering middle age, are we coming to
terms with being a good-enough philosopher and a good-
enough choreographer? To label our work either a success
or a failure would be an overstatement. Between the two
lies this vast terrain I like to call *the middling*, to which
almost everybody we know belongs. Growing up in the
1980s and 90s during the rise of neoliberalism, our nearly-
fanatical dedication as adults to making dances and writing
books, but also to each other, left little space for anything
else. For the past two decades, we were zealous entrepre-
neurs of our own selves. Yet Netta is much more connected
to her artistic community than I am to any intellectual circle. She has a seat at the table. I rarely leave my desk.

104.   I am more often exposed to and inspired by ex-
perimental performances than academic conferences. Witnessing Netta's daily practice, following her process from
first rehearsal to opening night, seeing her on stage: all
have been critical lessons that profoundly influenced my
thought. Whatever enabled her to make a life in art in-
formed the ways I pursue the life of the mind. For *Helga
and the Three Sailors*, she looped fragmented phrases of
her own movements as a child, excavated from hours of
home videos, which she then relearned to execute using
her highly trained adult body. This work of autochoreog-
raphy made the present notebook possible. But nothing
prepared me for our first collaboration, on her next piece,
Paramodernities, a series of six dance lectures dedicated
to key twentieth-century choreographers. At the end of
Halberstam's interview with Netta about this epic show
he brought up the fact that "your husband wrote and per-
formed" the text for the first installment. She replied that
the "friction between moving bodies and spoken ideas" evi-
dent throughout this performance is also a "kind of couples
therapy." It reminded me that, when we were in college, I
dreamt of the day we would open a joint school for philosophy and choreography, calling it *The Mind-Body Problem*.

105.   As for my work, the four books I have written
are not significant contributions to the established schol-
arly fields to which they only appear to belong. They are
a silent dialogue of me with myself, to borrow Arendt's
poetic formulation. Though I am considered an expert on
nothing, they are still all works in *Kishik Studies*. After the
fact, the autophilosophical tendencies of these books are
hard to miss. My publication record from the past dozen
years demonstrates little interest in developing a systematic thought or a coherent worldview. My goal — which I
see now as the overarching task of philosophy — has been
to articulate a form of life that must always be imagined
because it is never just a factual given. This is not world-
making but life-quilting. Since no one should be bothered
to write a critique of my body of work, I might as well accept my own challenge and conduct in these pages a short
self-study of my books. Such an attempt is not as odd as it
may sound. One of its precedents is Augustine's *Retractions*,
which is a detailed reassessment of all his previous texts.
Nietzsche's *Ecce Homo* also comes to mind. It is his last
work to be published during his lifetime, finished when he
was forty-four years old, which is my current age. Following
his lead, these pages are also an attempt to "tell my life to
myself."

106.   It is finally dawning on me that the present note-book could eventually be polished and published as either the preface or postface, intro or outro, for my book series. Hence this text can be read as either volume five or volume zero of *To Imagine a Form of Life*. The final installment in my loose pentalogy may also be visualized as the middle point in a quincunx, like the arrangement of the five dots on a dice. The first four volumes are the corners of a square, while this fifth element stands at its center. As a work of ex-perimental scholarship, the series grew stranger with each installment. As a *paraphilosophy*, it is to philosophy what Sancho Panza is to Don Quixote. However, I'm neither a loyal aid, nor do I pace the sidelines of the narrowing professional field. Instead, my deviant research yields com-plementary models, each set to investigate a facet of a form of life, which is indeed my own, though it is also an amal-gam of five very different encounters. Each volume looks at the emancipatory potential of some possibility of exist-ence, but only through a certain eye that, like every eye, has a specific blind spot that another eye, or the next book, compensates for. What links my suite of outré studies is not only one thing they all see, but different things each cannot see.

107.   I like to imagine my favorite thinkers locked inside a panopticon, Bentham's prison made of a circle of cells plus a central watchtower. Given the choice, where would they position themselves? The guard's platform in the tower is my educated guess, as it provides a sweeping overview of the multitude of inmates, who cannot look back to observe the observer. This also used to be my preferred place: the shadowy and unmoving center from which I gazed at whatever I was writing about. But can the watchtower be watched? My own little Copernican revolution came once I realized that my fields of research were peripheral platforms on which I stood looking in, directed at one central point. Each one of the previous installments gives a different perspective on the same thing, which only in this notebook, in retrospect, I can simply and finally call *myself*. Book covers are false advertisements: we assume that the author is going to write about what the title draws attention to. But what if the title is an observation ramp from which the author is to be seen? One good reason to write more than one book is that one's view of oneself better not be one-dimensional. More texts are like still cameras set in a circle, capturing a single gesture one after another, like Neo from *The Matrix* dodging a bullet.

108.   Why is it harder to write about my public work than my private life? This notebook was originally meant to be the space where I reflect on my previous studies. I wanted to take stock of a continuous project that began in earnest two decades ago — right after moving to New York, during a gap year before grad school — when I filled thirteen composition notebooks with my self-directed thoughts about the notion of life and its form. These juvenile ideas, even before getting channeled through my long-winded and far-flung investigations, already articulate some of the main concerns in my now virtually complete book series. *To Imagine a Form of Life* has been my passion project all along, though I've never engaged in more standard, specialized research — the kind of sad science that pleases the gods of academia but crushes the scholar's soul. Guntrip, however, has a point: "The schizoid fear of full self-committal accounts for much inability to concentrate attention in study." Each of my books is like a collection of sketches made while dwelling for a few years in a different quarter of the same city. In this sense the entire series resembles a thick personal album, with a reach that occasionally exceeds its grasp, and a dedicated tenacity that perfumes over the faint smell of resignation.

109.   Fairbairn also understood my approach to every book I ever finished: "To mitigate a sense of impoverishment following giving and creating, the individual with a schizoid component often employs an interesting defense. He adopts the attitude that what he has given or created is worthless." While composing this notebook, I already feel like a method actor: totally identifying with a role, suspending judgment, while knowing full well that I will soon shed its conceit, disengage, and move on to the next thing. I even write each of these daily notes as an isolated and dense microcosm, like Cornell's shadow boxes, though mine are made not of physical objects but entirely of quotes and thoughts. Once one page is done another is needed almost immediately. For years I've been following Nietzsche's advice to never take myself as seriously as I take my work, assuming that I'm just "the soil, sometimes the dung and manure on which, out of which, it grows." Now I know that the schizoid muck I've been shoveling in the real world is precisely the form of life that my abstract texts could barely imagine. I am the blind spot that remained unsaid in what was said. I am the axis around which my thought turns. I am an object lesson in the schizoid way of being. I am its proof of concept.

110.   When I turned thirty I completed *To Imagine a Language*, the first volume of *To Imagine a Form of Life*. But its kernel was already present a decade before, when, as an undergraduate student in Haifa, I became quite obsessed with Wittgenstein's work. I was particularly drawn to his repeated appeal to the notions of life and form of life, which made his whole understanding of language possible. Given the indeterminacy inherent in both speaking and living, his singular approach to the former enabled me to make radically new sense of the latter. But as I was mulling over the ethical thought behind his philosophy of life, its political implications left me cold. So another relation, between life and power, became the central concern of another book: *The Coming Politics*, however, is more than the second volume in my series. It is a consideration of the work to which my entire life project ultimately responds. In the fall of 2001, after a delay due to the attack on the World Trade Center, I attended two seminars each Tuesday: in the mornings with Agamben at Princeton and in the afternoons with Derrida at the New School. Sitting in these two rooms during that time, and then visiting Agamben for a long weekend in Venice, ensured that ever since his teachings shaped the bulk of my philosophical writings.

111.   Agamben begins with the figure of homo sacer and ends with his own notion of form-of-life; I begin with form of life and end with homo schizoid. He focuses on the power *over* life in its bare or naked state; I insist on the power *of* life with its myriad of inseparable forms. He views a camp called Auschwitz as the paradigm of modern biopolitics; I look in an altogether different direction to find a city called New York. This is where my thought turned. From the moment I laid my eyes on Benjamin's *Arcades Project*, his unfinished notebooks filled with quotations and reflections on Paris as the capital of the nineteenth century, I dreamt of using them as a template for a sprawling meditation on Manhattan, capital of the twentieth. The result was the third volume, *A Theory of a City*, my wild book of fictional philosophy. There was also a clandestine and nocturnal graffiti operation that followed on its heels. Of course, my Manhattan Project also had to be blind to its own lacuna, which led me to pivot from Benjamin's localized critical theory to Spinoza's globalized theology, from the culture of a city to the nature of the world, from the modern capital of man to the ancient kingdom of God, from an exemplary place to the origin of time, from life's fullness to its true bareness.

112.   *On the Rest of the World* is my winter book, assuming each of the four volumes reflects the mood of a consecutive season. I have felt cursed while working on this creative biblical commentary, and I still believe that there are shadowy forces who are displeased that my occult treatise saw the light of day. Paranoia aside, I am at peace with the heterodox ways in which I peeled away from Genesis 1–11 the endless layers of presuppositions about its meaning. Nevertheless, the argument of my latest book led me to conclude that it should be my last. This notebook is not so much another piece of work as a slightly idle look back. As a whole, *To Imagine a Form of Life* remains the phenomenology of my personal spirit. To imagine x (a language, a politics, a city, a world, a self) was a way to imagine my form of life. The full series, I realize now, functions like five figurative paintings (images of forms derived from life) in three scales (small, medium, large) and two orientations (portrait or landscape). But while the work on each installment was sparked by the discovery of its predecessor's blind spot, the bittersweet truth is that, for the first time in my career, as the present self study is nearing its end, I have no clue what my new research project might be.

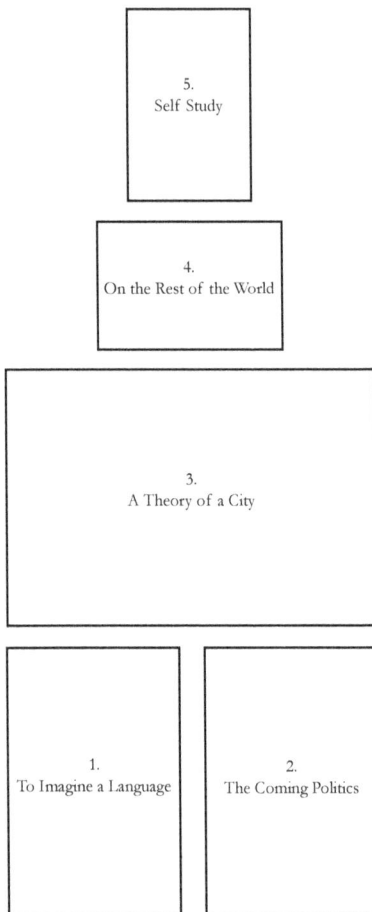

Figure 4.

113.   I recently wrote that "everyone in the pre-Abrahamic book exists, but only barely." Genesis is the most profound expression of loneliness, which might be the true essence of tragedy (rather than conflict). It holds true for humans as well as for God, who speaks volumes by telling Adam that it is not good to be alone. This sacred text perpetuates a schizoid dream that leads to a lonesome nightmare: the triumphant monotheistic view of God as an unchecked sovereign power assumes a divine subjectivity independent of any object. This is also Spinoza's monistic idea of an immanent substance that exists in itself and is conceived through itself, acting according to its own nature, limited by nothing. I had skin in the game when I depicted the Edenic state as childfree, linking it to God's role as a creator and molder of lives but not their father. Genesis, which can simply mean *birth*, is not a theogony. God has no offspring. And neither do I. The new counterculture slogan, I often tell my students, is *pass memes, not genes.* Or as Beauvoir replied to a kibbutz member who wondered whether she writes books because she doesn't have children, "Sir, do you have children because you don't write books?" Try holding a baby and a pen simultaneously, Nelson dares her readers.

114.   Why compare writing and birthing, reading and rearing? Will treating creative processes as labor pains solve a problem or duplicate it? If a piece of prose or a work of art often offers a glance into the past, then the child represents the future. Though always open to interpretation, what is experienced in a library, a museum, or a theater is a done deal. By facing on stage what is *no more*, the audience is propelled backwards, into the *not yet* behind the exit door, like Benjamin's angel of history. The innocent child's futurity, by contrast, can be an alibi that legitimizes the present conduct of cynical adults. This rhetoric, Edelman argues, allows politicians to speak in the name of, or act for the sake of, those symbolic children who are rarely asked what they really want. Winnicott, however, offers another way to draw the distinction between books and babies: "A mother and father do not produce a baby as an artist produces a picture or a potter a pot. They have started up a developmental process which results in there being a lodger in the mother's body and then in her arms and then in the home provided by the parents, and what this lodger will turn out to be like is outside anyone's control." This lodger might even grow up to eschew fatherhood to maintain said control.

115.   Knausgård's typical take on the subject: "Children were life, and who would turn their back on life? And writing, what else was it but death? Letters, what else were they but bones in a cemetery?" The cottage industry of contemporary autofiction thrives on this omnipresent tension between literary production and biological reproduction, recollection and procreation. A rare exception is *I Love Dick*, where neither Kraus's husband nor the eponymous Dick are there to impregnate her. Other specimens of this genre, plus this autophilosophy, reinforce the dual concern with the writer's prose and progeny. When an author holds a book and a book holds an author, even the mere notion of a needy baby eases this self-involved and self-referential death grip. Part of the allure of Nelson's *The Argonauts* is its implication that you can have it all: composing a queer text peppered with sophisticated theoretical references, while cloaking it in accessible and reassuring passages on the values of family life, she has anal sex on the first page and vaginal birth by the book's end. By contrast, the straight and sincere prose of Heti's *Motherhood* assumes that a binary choice must be made, as she narrates her tireless (or tiresome) inner struggle to its truly radical childfree conclusion.

116.   My exercise in life-writing is dedicated to the child who *never was*. Once I even thought of these notes as letters addressed to my hypothetical offspring, who might read them as an adult. But since I doubt he or she will ever exist, and since you, dear reader, have made a real effort to reach what is almost the end of this notebook, could you take up the figurative position of my child for just a second? Though what can I possibly pass along? Is it meaningful knowledge, or some minor traumas? And what am I left with, once my writings enter a world already oversaturated with so many texts? Am I even interested in books acting as letters exchanged between select friends? Who might these unknown friends be? Or do I write these notes especially for Netta, my first reader and best friend, as the window of parenting opportunity is closing in on us? So what am I trying to tell her here? What she already knows? That we are hoarding an excess of love we have nowhere to put? For her twentieth birthday, when she was a student in New York and I a soldier in Israel, she received in the mail the strangest of gifts: a box covered with a collage of photos of us as little kids, containing a baby blanket and a note that reads, *for our child to be.* It is still tucked away in our front closet.

117.   "Whether I want kids is the greatest secret I keep from myself." Like Heti, both Netta and I have been equally torn on this subject for far too long, going back and forth ad nauseam without ever reaching a definitive decision. Nothing was physiologically stopping us from conceiving. But whenever we said to ourselves that eventually we will make the leap, the part of us that didn't want it was still clearly expressed in our very actions, or the lack thereof. We communicated our wish to be childless by the ongoing fact of being childless. In so (not) doing, we effectively aborted the desire for parenthood. Somehow we were not persuaded by the overwhelming common sense that having children is the most important, satisfying, and meaningful aspect of adult life. But we were never at peace with our relatively carefree and self-centered existence. We recognized the narrowness of our monastic fidelity to choreography and philosophy. We felt deprived of the joys associated with raising kids. Were we simply afraid to face the difficulties and frustrations childrearing undoubtedly also entails? Did we consciously come to accept Euripides's conflicting claim that "the childless are happy in their misfortune"?

118.   In the book of Genesis, afterlife does not stand for what happens after death, but refers to one's existence *after giving life*. I have shown that the age of the earliest biblical characters is split in two: the first, prepartum age (from birth to the arrival of one's firstborn) marks this world and chronicles its history; the second, postpartum age (beginning with parenthood and ending with death) is the closest they ever get to the world thereafter. In dark times like our own, I cannot think of a better manifestation of trust in *this* world than bringing into it a new life. From experience, I also believe that there is no better manifestation of *mistrust* in the world than becoming a philosopher. The minority of great philosophers who were also good parents are curious amphibian creatures (from *amphi-bios*, Greek for *both lives*). Nevertheless, a child can sometimes also drive a wedge between a parent and the world. Heti again: "I resent the spectacle of all this breeding, which I see as a turning away from the living — an insufficient love for the rest of us, we billions of orphans already living." For a schizoid, the figure of the child can be a false promise of a new, true, full, or good relationship, one that will at last succeed where all other relations have failed.

119.   Besides the occasional flare-up, my schizoid demon remains under control most of the time. What gives it away no matter what, its biggest win over my sense of self, is the simple fact that I am childless. There are many convincing ways to explain how this situation transpired, above all Netta's own reluctance to become a mother, for reasons partly different than mine. But more and more I attribute my personal fate to the force of this malicious demon who implores: don't be weak and vulnerable, you have no need for anything or anybody else, stay impenetrable and unyielding, nothing should change for better or worse, contentment is to be avoided as much as misery, minimize friction and maximize stability. Fairbairn: "Childbirth signifies not so much the gain of a child, but loss of contents with resulting emptiness." Question: can a schizoid with child be compared to a gay person stuck in a heterosexual marriage? Being childfree is a form of life, just like being a philosopher. If these are schizoid triumphs then so be it. This is who I am, or what I have become, and I am not alone. Such lives cannot be reduced to an aberration that should be uprooted. It feels wrong to speak of those who weren't "fortunate" enough to become parents, or those who "unfortunately" became philosophers.

120.   "Being a father is a rather abstract business." Coetzee made me wonder if only a mother is able to achieve the ultimate object relation with another person who has emerged from her self. Could men be more prone to develop schizoid tendencies because of this inherent lack? And yet Freud insists for some odd reason that the woman is the one who lacks something so fundamental as a phallus. If anything, it is I who feel castrated for not having a child, not being a father, not experiencing this incomparable relationship with someone who wouldn't be if not for me and whose ontological security hinges on my daily actions. Yet fatherhood, like sovereignty and divinity, whether it is symbolic, imaginary, or real, entails this power over life that is not necessarily benevolent. As a grown man, not-yet-being-a-father is one salient stance that suspends or at least defers the operation of the patriarchal apparatus that can "capture, orient, determine, intercept, model, control, or secure the gestures, behaviors, opinions, or discourses of living beings." But while Agamben, in this passage, focuses on lives being subjected to some power, and while Lacan would insist on the paternal provenance of said power, I am interested in the opposite perspective: the ways my life unfolds *in the name of the child*, the one that never was.

121.   Kierkegaard's letters to his fiancée "make it clear that their author was to become not a husband but a writer." Like a castrato, he sacrificed erotic love for art. In order to philosophize, Regine had to remain his phantom wife, not a lawfully wedded one. I've been harboring analogous feelings toward my potential progeny, which Heti echoes: "I know the more I think about having a child, the more that creates the figure of the child who is not born. The more I write this, the more this not-born child becomes a real thing, a figure *not there*, a specific person who is being denied life." Today, as my speculative child is shifting from the realm of possibilities to that of missed opportunities, anticipation and trepidation are giving way to regret and mourning. But how can I mourn what I never had? For this purpose Freud reserved the adjacent concept of melancholia: an imaginative capacity to make the unobtainable or unknowable appear as if it has been lost. Losing an external loved object (like the death of Aristotle's son Nicomachus) prompts in the mourner a regressive reaction. But the melancholic precedes this loss with a pre-emptive tragic simulation, like my recurrent fantasy of a child who never was. Yet I am the one who is lost in this whole constellation, lamenting the life I never had.

122.   I have said here little or nothing about my by and large happy childhood, my dear brother and sister, my brilliant school friends, and the serene community surrounded by the harsh country where we all grew up; or the loving and stable household my mom maintained next door to the small electronics assembly line that my dad managed, where I worked as a teenager; or the colorful cast of adult relatives, neighbors, and teachers; or the endless hours playing soccer, playing music, playing by and with myself. What prevented my good memories from finding their way into these pages? Since I am not a father, there are ways in which I never stopped being a child. But this also explains why I don't have much access to my younger self. Given that the child lives on in the adult, Laplanche thinks that a parent facing their child "is involved in a relationship with his other self, with the other he once was. The child in front of him brings out the child within him." The child I once was is lost to the father I can hardly imagine becoming. So as the years are passing, my inner child is slowly taken away from me, although I constantly fight for custody over it, often by playing with my niece or nephews who, like most kids I happen to interact with, surprisingly warm up to me pretty quickly.

123.   To keep the option of pregnancy open, before this door will be shut by a hormone treatment that should lower the risk of breast cancer recurrence, Netta's doctor asked us to consider in vitro fertilization. After our insurance agreed to cover the IVF cost, we hesitatingly decided to give it a shot. So last Christmas Day we found ourselves seated in the empty waiting room of a medical office near Columbus Circle. Netta's cycle, clinically enhanced and closely monitored, determined that our immaculate conception had to happen on that particular morning, when her eggs and my sperm were first extracted from our bodies in separate rooms, using very different techniques, and then combined in a lab. On New Year's Eve, as we were walking down Fifth Avenue after leaving the Metropolitan Museum high on MDMA, we received an email informing us that a single healthy female embryo survived the procedure. It has been waiting for us in its frozen state of limbo ever since. At our age, with the odds against us, a failed IVF would have eased the endless parenthood conundrum (while giving us some peace of mind, knowing that at least we tried). Which is why the tidings about our good luck so far are only making me feel more perturbed than ever before. We exist in a holding pattern.

124.   I was hoping this notebook would give me some clarity about the nagging question of the child, a clarity that is much needed at this moment in my life. Not long after I will reach its final page, a decision about transferring the embryo from vitro to utero, from laboratory to Yerushalmy, will have to be made. At the time of writing, I honestly do not know whether or when we will go ahead with the procedure. Even if we do, there is a serious chance that it will end in miscarriage. If so, I don't want us to go through this treatment again. But then what? Repeating small variations of the same life we have been pursuing so far until one of us dies and then the other? Can we continue to be alone in New York while our families are growing older in Israel? Will choreography and philosophy keep holding us like they did in the past? Have I reached here the limit of my thought? Am I settling into the trivial life of an average academic? Why invest in yet another volume in the series? Why write what will most likely be read by so few? Can I continue, like Nietzsche, to "live on my own credit"? And since it is patently true that "a book is not supposed to be a mirror" but a door, then what is waiting for me on the other side? Or do certain types of mirrors function like different kinds of doors?

125.   There are eleven blank pages left in this notebook. It began with the two words jotted on its cover — *Book Ends* — sensing that this was the right place and time to bookend my thought, tie up loose ends, and bring everything to a close. Put together, the five volumes I produced are as long as Joyce's *Ulysses*. But only now, hundreds of thousands of lesser words in, I feel pressed to articulate a basic truth which I held to be self-evident all along: to be human is to imagine one's form by living it with others. The most elementary human world consists of overlapping ways of being (traditions, customs, habits, fashions, et cetera) that we practice or critique, change or conserve, struggle with or even die for. Nothing distills the fundamental meaning of our being better than these forms. To imagine anything we might consider of import — happiness or health, liberty or equality, truth or knowledge, solidarity or individuality, power or beauty, animality or divinity, race or nationality, class or sexuality — is to conceive a form of life into which such notions are woven, where they make theoretical and practical sense. And no religious, artistic, economic, political, sociological, or psychological consideration can reduce the complicated network of criss-crossing forms to its limited discursive field.

126.   This is my form of life. What's yours? On the one hand, an autophilosophy feels like an easy text to write, since I happen to know its subject matter inside and out, and can instantly tell whether each sentence rings true or not. On the other hand, Wittgenstein is always right: "Nothing is so difficult as not deceiving oneself." But who could legitimately tell whether this notebook is a convoluted act of self-deception? As I said from the start, I wrote it for myself and for strangers. Neither, it stands to reason, can adequately judge me. It is worth stressing, however, that I'm presently uncertain whether these words will ever get published or find an audience. Does this text serve a greater good, or was it composed under the presumption that I cannot help anyone and no one can help me? My endeavor can feel like an open gate that only I can ever enter. Meanwhile, I'm starting to realize that my previously published books were more like notebooks for personal use only. But if the first four volumes were perpetual drafts for a real book yet to be written, maybe this fifth and last one—the one vertiginously revolving around me—is a roundabout way to finally face other people, without vying for recognition, and without trying to fix anything, or anyone, not even myself.

127.   "Judgments, judgments of value, concerning life, for it or against it, can, in the end, never be true; they have value only as symptoms, they are worthy of consideration only as symptoms; in themselves such judgments are stupidities. One must by all means stretch out one's fingers and make the attempt to grasp this amazing finesse, that *the value of life cannot be estimated.*" What, then, does *To Imagine a Form of Life* end up saying about me, since Nietzsche insists that it can say nothing valuable about life as such? Underneath it all, the complete series tells the story of an author grappling with his crippling mind and facing his looming irrelevance by working on a handful of increasingly brazen and baffling studies that culminated in a philosophy of himself. It ultimately made him see why the best public service befitting his peculiar position is to stop bothering the public after these notes reach their conclusion. Yet reading my work is only one way to know me. There are others: visit my apartment, watch me dance. Anyhow, while this notebook describes the bottle in which I am trapped like a confused fly, its aim is to show the insect a way out of this glass-house. Will I be able to stop doing autophilosophy when I want to, or will the schizoid picture keep holding me captive?

128. My year of schizoid thinking happened to coincide with the precise moment in history this personal psychopathology expanded overnight, with the plague's onslaught, into a new social norm of global proportions. All along, the notebook felt like a work of crisis, in the Greek sense of *krisis*: the turning point of a disease or a medical procedure, when a decision about the life or death of a patient is being made. I mean it not physically but spiritually: it is not the fact but the form of my life that, like the form of this world, might be collapsing in on itself. Is this why I sense that the only logical course of action is to finish this notebook and retire from writing? Ultimately, homo schizoid does not relate but retreats. Instead of new branches, I might grow deeper roots. Guntrip: "The schizoid has withdrawn from the outer world and the future, and in doing so turns back, regresses to the inner world where the past is enshrined." So should I just reread and rewrite what I've already written? What was never written must remain so. Proverbs: "In an intelligent mind wisdom rests. Among fools it makes itself known." The Talmud explains this verse by invoking the *kish kish* sound a few coins make in an empty jug. My empty self has made enough noise. It is high time to remain silent.

129.   Goethe and his Werther, Mann and his Kröger, Rilke and his Brigge: strong, recognized artists dedicated their *Künstlerromane* to the struggles of lesser, imaginary artists. The same holds for Knausgård, Lerner, and Heti, only that their autofictional protagonists are earlier and feebler versions of their celebrated authorial selves. My autophilosophy is slightly different. Its main thesis: This is not working, and not for lack of trying. If my strategy so far was to seek redemption through writing, now I am looking for ways to be saved *from* writing. Too late, I'm sensing that to perpetuate my vocation is to wear out my welcome, as I clearly had plenty of good opportunities to have my say. Maybe Kafka is too dramatic when he wants a book to be the "axe for the frozen sea inside us." But I'm certain that the effect of my publications cannot be measured by the job I hold as a professor or the institutional fold into which I was admitted. My academic position is not a trustworthy testament to my contribution to philosophy. If only I could afford to add here a resignation letter from my college to make this point even clearer, the project of rendering myself irrelevant would be complete. There are times when the cessation of work proves itself to be a greater achievement than the work itself.

130.   *Speaking* the truth with a capital T is an infrequent event in my life. I only know how to approximate it through very slow writing, deliberately planned and meticulously edited. Since this notebook is like a vise that clamps my four books together, or their capstone, I also see it as a distillation of a distillation of my truth. But while a freer version of myself scares me, this hyper-controlled record no longer impresses me. When all is said and done, there is so little life left here to embrace. By the end the philosopher, like the emperor, tends to be naked. Yet it still pains me that most people who know me personally can't be bothered to read my work, as abstruse as it may be. And so I retreat back into these notes, this Hail Mary to prove my self-worth, only to realize that my true disappointment is clearly not with others but primarily with myself. Hence, instead of the final scene in a film, this notebook stands for the gesture of turning the house lights on while the credits are still rolling. There must be other ideas to explore, deeper things to understand, but I, personally, am resolved to put this venture behind me. Nevertheless, my friend Gil's reaction to these frustrations during a stroll in Central Park was spot on: "The lady doth protest too much."

131.   My stake in the ethos of life as literature is shrinking. My shockingly small private library doesn't reflect well on a genuine love for reading and writing. When I used to sit at the New York Public Library, before the pandemic shut it down, there were times when I couldn't think of one title to request from the stacks. Other times I believed I was writing the text I desired to read. But by now I no longer know what to make of the very medium of the printed book. At the same time, billions of written words are endlessly moving and fading on screens, instead of staying static or passive on paper. Yesterday Agamben posted online a piece comparing contemporary humanity to dwellers of a house on fire, only that these new flames are digital, invisible, and cold. While book writers are not the best firefighters against these virtual flames, they do possess one quality that Yu-jin, an empathetic colleague at my school, made me appreciate one evening over beer after class: "Patience is the only quality that ultimately separates the winners from the losers, and guarantees a kind of heaven on earth. For the impatient — those who cannot wait, those destined to eternal disappointment — there is no noticeable distinction between this world and hell."

132.   Winnicott: "In the artist of all kinds I think one can detect an inherent dilemma, which belongs to the co-existence of two trends, the urgent need to communicate and the still more urgent need not to be found. This might account for the fact that we cannot conceive of an artist's coming to the end of the task that occupies his whole nature." Nothing is stopping me from getting another empty notebook after this one fills up and adding more notes for much longer, like Penelope's weaving or Scheherazade's storytelling. My exercise has no natural end. It can only be abandoned, for reasons that may or may not have to do with the prospects of fatherhood. For the past nineteen weeks I was not only withdrawing into a personal inner world. Like the mystic, I was also retreating to a place where I could "communicate secretly with subjective objects and phenomena." According to Winnicott, this loss of contact with the shared reality was being balanced out by a gain in terms of feeling real. A fragmentary notebook is such an ideal conduit for philosophers who, like artists and mystics, operate in a transitional space that allows them to shuttle back and forth between being known and being unknown to themselves as well as to others; lost and found and lost again.

133.   If I were to postpone reaching the end of this notebook, the work that saturated my days for more than eighteen years would extend a tiny bit longer. It is not quite clear what I will do with myself once I finish this autophilosophy and complete the final volume in the series. While I am no longer pressed to replicate my existence thus far by writing more books, I am also unsure how to set the conditions for the remainder of my life. After all these years, I can begin to discern for the first time the general outline of my own philosophy, right as I prepare to terminate my efforts. Even though I do not intend to flesh it out by producing new content, I have founded for this purpose the Institute for Kishik Studies, to promote research into my nebulous lifework. Inaugurated in a modest ceremony attended by myself, I am the institute's sole member, doubling as its tireless director and leading scholar. This arrangement entails lots of administrative paperwork, but it will hopefully start to pay off once this notebook turns into the first publication written with the institute's generous support. This sounds like a joke, but I'm dead serious about the urgent need in today's critical climate to develop a new field of research that I would like to call *self studies.*

134.   Next, my institute is prepared to launch its own press, called Vanity Press. Once I had a dream to open a place where every morning authors will print and bind copies of their previously-published books, and then personally sell them in the afternoon to interested readers. This absurd take on self-publishing was meant to be a small way to combat the alienation of intellectual labor, by offering occupational therapy for jaded writers. This imaginary enterprise matured today into a real decision to turn my five volumes into a complete omnibus edition that will be neither printed nor typed but actually handwritten from start to finish in ten notebooks, just like this one. David, the Scrivener, could produce a limited run of this non-fungible philosophy. It would mark the sixth time I have refocused my practice: veering from analytic to continental thought, from urban to religious studies, from psychoanalytic theory to performance art. It is one thing to write what you want to read; it is another to write what you will copy again and again. This is *amor fati intellectualis*. There is no more appropriate vocation for the dark age ahead than that of a scribe or a *sofer*, replicating with devotion words first composed when the sun still rose, at least from where I happen to stand.

135.   I finished writing my first book while living for a few months in Tel Aviv, where I have recently arrived to conclude the work on my last. Then I was wondering about the world and life being one. Now I am asking how subject and object can enter a zone of indetermination where knowing thyself means letting the ego go, dissolving into what Freud calls an *oceanic feeling*, which is not unlike the emptying of the subject that Christians call *kenosis*, or the rejection of the soul as substance that Buddhists call *anatman*. Hence Didion on the affinity of geology and psychology: "A hill is a transitional accommodation to stress, and ego may be a similar accommodation." Since this note is the final shard of my sense of self, I will soon merge with the waves that kept breaking while these words were being written, first by the East River and then by the Mediterranean Sea. As for the rest of this page, it is intentionally left blank.

Figure 5.

NOTES

1. Ludwig Wittgenstein, *Culture and Value* (Chicago: University of Chicago Press, 2006). Jean Laplanche, "Time and the Other," in Laplanche, *Essays on Otherness* (London: Routledge, 1999). Rainer Maria Rilke and Lou Andreas-Salomé, *Rilke and Andreas-Salomé: A Love Story in Letters* (New York: Norton, 2008). Lionel Ziprin, *Songs for Schizoid Siblings* (New York: The Song Cave, 2017).

2. Michel Foucault, *The Care of the Self* (New York: Vintage, 1990). Edward McGushin, *Foucault's Askesis: An Introduction to the Philosophical Life* (Evanston, IL: Northwestern University Press, 2007). Augustine, *Confessions* (Oxford: Oxford University Press, 1991). Michel de Montaigne, "Experience," in Montaigne, *Selected Essays* (Indianapolis, IN: Hackett, 2012).

3. René Descartes, *Discourse on Method and Meditations on First Philosophy* (Indianapolis, IN: Hackett, 2010). Friedrich Nietzsche, *On the Genealogy of Morals and Ecce Homo* (New York: Vintage, 2010). Hannah Arendt, *Love and Saint Augustine* (Chicago: University of Chicago Press, 2014).

4. Hans Blumenberg, *Shipwreck with Spectator: Paradigm of a Metaphor for Existence* (Cambridge, MA: MIT Press, 2013). Ralph Waldo Emerson, "The American Scholar," in Emerson, *The Essential Writings* (New York: Modern Library, 2000). Stanley Cavell, *Little Did I Know: Excerpts from Memory* (Stanford, CA: Stanford University Press, 2010).

5. Michel Foucault, "The Hermeneutics of the Subject," in Foucault, *Ethics: Subjectivity and Truth* (New York: New Press, 1997). Theodor Adorno, *Minima Moralia: Reflections from Damaged Life* (London: Verso, 2005). Roland Barthes, *Roland Barthes* (Berkeley: University of California Press, 1994).

6. Ludwig Binswanger, "The Case of Lola Voss," in *Being-in-the-World: Selected Papers of Ludwig Binswanger* (New York: Basic Books, 1963). Donald W. Winnicott, "Ego Integration and Child Development," in Winnicott, *The Maturational Processes and the Facilitating Environment* (Abingdon: Routledge, 2018). R. D. Laing, *The Divided Self: An Existential Study in Sanity and Madness* (London: Penguin, 2010).

8. *Yedioth Ahronoth*, 4 February 1969. *Davar*, 5 February 1969. Sara Ahmed, *Living a Feminist Life* (Durham, NC: Duke University Press, 2017).

9. Yiyun Li, *Dear Friend, from My Life I Write to You in Your Life* (London: Penguin, 2018). Michel Foucault, *Subjectivity and Truth: Lectures at the Collège de France, 1980–1981* (London: Palgrave, 2016).

10. Roy Ben-Shai, private communication. Lauren Berlant, *Cruel Optimism* (Durham, NC: Duke University Press, 2012).

11. Originally published as: *Wittgenstein's Form of Life* (London: Continuum, 2008), *The Power of Life: Agamben and the Coming Politics* (Stanford, CA: Stanford University Press, 2011), *The Manhattan Project: A Theory of a City* (Stanford, CA: Stanford University Press, 2015), *The Book of Shem: On Genesis Before Abraham* (Stanford, CA: Stanford University Press, 2018). Wittgenstein, *Culture and Value*.

12. Paul B. Preciado, *Testo Junkie: Sex, Drugs, and Biopolitics in the Pharmacopornographic Era* (New York: The Feminist Press, 2013). Laing, *The Divided Self*. Nietzsche, *On the Genealogy of Morals*.

13. Eugen Bleuler, *Dementia Praecox; or, The Group of Schizophrenias* (New York: International Universities Press, 1950). Franz Kafka, "The Burrow," in Kafka, *The Complete Stories* (New York: Schocken, 1946). Franz Kafka, *The Blue Octavo Notebooks* (Cambridge, MA: Exact Change, 1991).

14. Laing, *The Divided Self*. György Lukács, *Soul & Form* (New York: Columbia University Press, 2010).

15. Herman Melville, "Bartleby the Scrivener," in Melville, *Billy Budd, Sailor, and Other Stories* (London: Penguin, 1985). Arthur Schopenhauer, "Similes, Parables, and Fables," in Schopenhauer, *Parerga and Paralipomena* (Oxford: Clarendon, 2010).

16. Donald W. Winnicott, "Communicating and Not Communicating," in *The Collected Works of D. W. Winnicott*, 12 vols (Oxford: Oxford University Press, 2016), VI: 1960–63. Ernst Kretschmer, *Physique and Character* (London: Routledge, 1999).

17. Harry Guntrip, *Schizoid Phenomena, Object Relations and the Self* (London: Routledge, 1992). W. R. D. Fairbairn, *Psychoanalytic Studies of the Personality* (London: Routledge, 1952).

18. Guntrip, *Schizoid Phenomena*. Jean-Paul Sartre, *No Exit* (New York: Vintage, 1989).

19. Harry Guntrip, *Personal Relations Therapy* (London: Aronson, 1994).

20. Fairbairn, *Psychoanalytic Studies.*

21. Slavoj Žižek, *How to Read Lacan* (New York: Norton, 2007). James Baldwin, "Letter from a Region of My Mind," in Baldwin, *The Fire Next Time* (New York: Penguin, 1990). Elizabeth Young-Bruehl, *Hannah Arendt: For Love of the World* (New Haven, CT: Yale University Press, 1982).

22. Edward S. Casey, "Being on Edge and Falling Apart," in Casey, *The World on Edge* (Bloomington: Indiana University Press, 2017). Fairbairn, *Psychoanalytic Studies.*

23. Olivia Laing, *The Lonely City: Adventures in the Art of Being Alone* (New York: Picador, 2016). Guntrip, *Personal Relations Therapy.*

24. Søren Kierkegaard, *Papers and Journals* (London: Penguin, 2015).

25. Søren Kierkegaard, *The Concept of Irony* (Princeton, NJ: Princeton University Press, 1992). Friedrich Nietzsche, *The Gay Science* (Cambridge: Cambridge University Press, 2001).

26. Epictetus, *Discourses, Fragments, Handbook* (Oxford: Oxford University Press, 2014). Gilles Deleuze, *The Logic of Sense* (New York: Columbia University Press, 1989). Nancy Sherman, *Stoic Warriors: The Ancient Philosophy Behind the Military Mind* (Oxford: Oxford University Press, 2005). Marcus Aurelius, *Meditations* (New York: Random House, 2003). *The Stoics Reader: Selected Writings and Tes-*

timonia, ed. by Brad Inwood and Lloyd Gerson (Indianapolis, IN: Hackett, 2008).

27. Alexandre Kojève, *Introduction to the Reading of Hegel* (Ithaca, NY: Cornell University Press, 1980). G. W. F. Hegel, *Phenomenology of Spirit* (Oxford: Oxford University Press, 1977). Blaise Pascal, *Pensées* (London: Penguin, 1995).

28. Boethius, *The Consolation of Philosophy* (Cambridge, MA: Harvard University Press, 2008). Nietzsche, *On the Genealogy of Morals.*

29. Kishik, *The Power of Life.*

30. Adrian Piper, "Food for the Spirit (1971)," in Piper, *Out of Order, Out of Sight* (Cambridge, MA: MIT Press, 1996). Lauren Fournier, *Autotheory as Feminist Practice in Art, Writing, and Criticism* (Cambridge, MA: MIT Press, 2021).

31. Guntrip, *Schizoid Phenomena.*

32. Kishik, *The Manhattan Project.*

33. Simone Weil, *First and Last Notebooks* (Oxford: Oxford University Press, 1970). Kishik, *The Book of Shem.*

34. Giorgio Agamben, *The Use of Bodies* (Stanford, CA: Stanford University Press, 2016). Giorgio Agamben, *The Open: Man and Animal* (Stanford, CA: Stanford University Press,

2012). Giorgio Agamben, *Infancy and History: The Destruction of Experience* (London: Verso, 2007). William Watkin, *Agamben and Indifference* (London: Rowman & Littlefield, 2014).

35. Louis Sass, "Deep Disquietudes: Reflections on Wittgenstein as Antiphilosopher," in *Wittgenstein: Biography and Philosophy*, ed. by James C. Klagge (Cambridge: Cambridge University Press, 2001). Ludwig Wittgenstein, *Private Notebooks: 1914–1916* (New York: Liveright, 2022). On Fairbairn's moral defense, see entry 20.

36. Gilles Deleuze and Félix Guattari, *Anti-Oedipus: Capitalism and Schizophrenia* (London: Continuum, 1983). Guntrip, *Schizoid Phenomena*. Donald W. Winnicott, "The Theory of the Parent-Infant Relationship," in Winnicott, *The Maturational Processes*. Jay Greenberg and Stephen Mitchell, *Object Relations in Psychoanalytic Theory* (Cambridge, MA: Harvard University Press, 1983).

37. Guntrip, *Schizoid Phenomena*. Greenberg and Mitchell, *Object Relations*.

38. W. R. D. Fairbairn, "Synopsis of an Object-Relations Theory of the Personality," *The International Journal of Psychoanalysis*, 44.2 (1963).

40. Greenberg and Mitchell, *Object Relations*.

42. Agamben, *Infancy and History*. Donald Winnicott, "Fear of Breakdown," *International Review of Psycho-Analysis*, 1.1–2 (1974).

43. Winnicott, "Fear of Breakdown." Giorgio Agamben, *Stanzas: Word and Phantasm in Western Culture* (Minneapolis: University of Minnesota Press, 1993).

44. Winnicott, "Communicating and Not Communicating." Guntrip, *Schizoid Phenomena*. Robert Stolorow, *Faces in a Cloud: Intersubjectivity in Personality Theory* (Northvale, NJ: Aronson, 1993).

45. On Fairbairn's moral defense, see entry 20. Guntrip, *Schizoid Phenomena*.

46. Guntrip, *Schizoid Phenomena*. Pascal, *Pensées*.

47. Guntrip, *Schizoid Phenomena*.

48. Roy Ben-Shai, *Moral Pathology* (unpublished dissertation, 2011).

50. Frantz Fanon, *Black Skin, White Masks* (London: Pluto Press, 1986).

51. Aristotle, *The Politics*, in *The Basic Works of Aristotle* (New York: Random House, 1941). Hannah Arendt, *The Origins of Totalitarianism* (London: Penguin, 2017).

52. Steven DeCaroli, "The Idea of Awakening: Giorgio Agamben and the Nagarjuna," *Res Publica*, 28 (2012). Giorgio Agamben, *The Idea of Prose* (Albany: State University of New York Press, 1995).

53. Walt Whitman, "Song of Myself," in Whitman, *Poetry and Prose*, ed. by Justin Kaplan (New York: Library of America, 1982).

54. Li, *Dear Friend*. Martin Heidegger, *Being and Time* (Albany: State University of New York Press, 1996). Judith Butler, *Precarious Life: The Powers of Mourning and Violence* (London: Verso, 2004). Judith Halberstam, "The Anti-Social Turn in Queer Studies," *Graduate Journal of Social Science*, 5.2 (2008). Mari Ruti, *The Ethics of Opting Out: Queer Theory's Defiant Subjects* (New York: Columbia University Press, 2017). Frank B. Wilderson, *Afropessimism* (New York: Liverlight, 2020).

55. Jean-Luc Nancy, "Abandoned Being," in Nancy, *The Birth to Presence* (Stanford, CA: Stanford University Press, 2009). Giorgio Agamben, *The Use of Bodies*.

56. Giorgio Agamben, "On the Uses and Disadvantages of Living among Specters," in Agamben, *Nudities* (Stanford, CA: Stanford University Press, 2010).

57. Laing, *The Divided Self.*

58. Giorgio Agamben, *Remnants of Auschwitz: The Witness and the Archive* (New York: Zone Books, 2000). Melanie Klein, "Notes on Some Schizoid Mechanisms," *International Journal of Psycho-Analysis*, 27 (1946).

59. Yossi Triest, "Corona-Time Notes: The Virus of Horror," *The Tavistock Institute*, March 2020 <https://tavinstitute. org/projects/corona-time-notes-the-virus-of-horror> [accessed 2 October 2022]. Kishik, *The Manhattan Project*. Giorgio Agamben, "Biosecurity and Politics," in Agamben, *Where Are We Now?* (London: ERIS, 2021).

61. Nietzsche, *Ecce Homo*. Gilles Deleuze and Félix Guattari, *What Is Philosophy?* (London: Verso, 2015). Deleuze and Guattari, *Anti-Oedipus*.

62. Sylvère Lotringer and David Morris, *Schizo-Culture* (Pasadena, CA: Semiotext(e), 2014). Louis Sass, *The Paradoxes of Delusion: Wittgenstein, Schreber, and the Schizophrenic Mind* (Ithaca, NY: Cornell University Press, 1994).

63. Louis Sass, *Madness and Modernism: Insanity in the Light of Modern Art, Literature, and Thought* (Oxford: Oxford University Press, 2017). Nancy McWilliams, "Some Thoughts about Schizoid Dynamics," *The Psychoanalytic Review*, 93.1 (2006). Nancy McWilliams, "Schizoid Personality," in McWilliams, *Psychoanalytic Diagnosis* (New York: Guilford Press, 2011).

64. Sass, "Deep Disquietudes."

65. Yoel Hoffmann, *The Idea of Self, East and West: A Comparison between Buddhist Philosophy and the Philosophy of David Hume* (Calcutta: K.L.M, 1980).

66. George Devereux, *Basic Problems of Ethnopsychiatry* (Chicago: University of Chicago Press, 1980).

67. Peter Sloterdijk, *In the World Interior of Capital: For a Philosophical Theory of Globalization* (Cambridge: Polity, 2014). Guy Debord, *The Society of the Spectacle* (New York: Zone Books, 2012).

68. Alan Turing, "Computing Machinery and Intelligence," *Mind*, 59 (October 1950). Sherry Turkle, *Alone Together: Why We Expect More from Technology and Less from Each Other* (New York: Basic Books, 2017).

69. Weil, *First and Last Notebooks.* Karen Horney, "Resignation: the Appeal of Freedom," in Horney, *Neurosis and Human Growth: The Struggle Toward Self-Realization* (New York: Norton, 1950). David Foster Wallace, "E Unibus Pluram," in Wallace, *A Supposedly Fun Thing I'll Never Do Again* (New York: Little, Brown and Company, 1997).

70. Amba Azaad, "The Malignant Melancholy," *The New Inquiry,* 29 January 2018 <https://thenewinquiry.com/the-malignant-melancholy> [accessed 29 September 2022].

71. Emanuele Coccia, "Reversing the New Global Monasticism," *Fall Semester*, 21 April 2020 <https://fallsemester.org/2020-1/2020/4/17/emanuele-coccia-escaping-the-global-monasticism> [accessed 22 July 2022].

72. Foucault, "The Hermeneutics of the Subject." Michel Foucault, *The Government of Self and Others: Lectures at the Collège de France, 1982–1983* (London: Palgrave Macmillan, 2010).

73. Claire Bishop, *Artificial Hells: Participatory Art and the Politics of Spectatorship* (London: Verso, 2012).

74. Natasha Stagg, *Sleeveless: Fashion, Image, Media, New York 2011–2019* (Pasadena, CA: Semiotext(e), 2017). Mami Suwa and Kunifumi Suzuki, "The Phenomenon of 'Hikikomori' (Social Withdrawal) and the Socio-cultural Situation in Japan Today," *Journal of Psychopathology*, 19 (2013).

75. Paul B. Preciado, *Pornotopia: An Essay on Playboy's Architecture and Biopolitics* (New York: Zone Books, 2014). Paul B. Preciado, "Learning from the Virus," *Artforum*, May/June 2020.

76. Karl Ove Knausgård, *My Struggle: Book Six* (New York: Farrar, Straus and Giroux, 2018).

77. Nicholas Dames, "The New Fiction of Solitude," *The Atlantic*, April 2016. David Hume, *The Private Correspondence of David Hume* (London: Henry Colburn, 1820).

78. Kishik, *The Manhattan Project.*

79. Donald Winnicott, "Creativity and its Origins," in Winnicott, *Playing and Reality* (New York: Routledge, 2005).

80. Daniel Heller-Roazen, *The Inner Touch: Archaeology of a Sensation* (New York: Zone Books, 2007). Oliver Sacks, "The Disembodied Lady," in Sacks, *The Man Who Mistook His Wife for a Hat* (London: Picador, 2015). Giorgio Agamben, "The Friend," in Agamben, *What Is an Apparatus? and Other Essays* (Stanford, CA: Stanford University Press, 2009).

81. Jeffrey Seinfeld, *The Empty Core: An Object Relations Approach to the Psychotherapy of the Schizoid Personality* (Northvale, NJ: Aronson, 1991).

83. Jacques Lacan, *The Object Relation: The Seminar of Jacques Lacan, Book IV* (Cambridge: Polity, 2021).

84. Jacques-Alain Miller, "A Fantasy," *Lacanian Praxis*, 1.11 (2005). Franz Kafka, *The Complete Novels: The Trial, America, the Castle* (London: Vintage, 2008). Lacan, *The Object Relation.*

85. Pascal, *Pensées*. Lacan, *The Object Relation*.

86. Lacan, *The Object Relation*. Jessica Benjamin, *Beyond Doer and Done to: Recognition Theory, Intersubjectivity and the Third* (London: Routledge, 2017).

87. Donald Winnicott, "The Use of an Object and Relating through Identification," in Winnicott, *Playing and Reality*.

88. Donald Winnicott, "Transitional Objects and Transitional Phenomena," in Winnicott, *Playing and Reality*. Lacan, *The Object Relation*.

89. Ludwig Bolk, "On the Problem of Anthropogenesis," *Proceedings of the Royal Academy, Amsterdam*, 29 (1926). Giorgio Agamben, "What is an Act of Creation," in Agamben, *The Fire and the Tale* (Stanford, CA: Stanford University Press, 2017). Winnicott, "Creativity and its Origins."

90. Lacan, *The Object Relation*.

91. Jeffery M. Masson, "Freud and the Seduction Theory," *The Atlantic*, February 1984. Jean Laplanche, "The Unfinished Copernican Revolution," in Laplanche, *Essays on Otherness*.

92. Salvador Dalí, *Madonna*, 1958, Metropolitan Museum of Art, New York.

93. R. D. Laing, *Knots* (New York: Pantheon, 1970).

94. Richard Avedon and James Baldwin, *Nothing Personal* (New York: Atheneum, 1964). Plato, *Alcibiades*, in *Plato: Complete Works* (Indianapolis, IN: Hackett, 1997).

95. Guntrip, *Schizoid Phenomena*. Augustine, *Confessions*.

96. Kishik, *The Book of Shem*. Augustine, *Confessions*. Arendt, *Love and Saint Augustine*.

97. Laing, *Knots*.

98. Sigmund Freud, "The Neuro-Psychoses of Defence," in *The Standard Edition of the Complete Psychological Works of Sigmund Freud*, 24 vols (London: Hogarth, 1953–74), III: *Early Psychoanalytic Publications (1893–1899)* (1962). Fairbairn, *Psychoanalytic Studies*. Maggie Nelson, *Bluets* (Seattle, WA: Wave Books, 2009).

101. Chris Kraus, *I Love Dick* (Pasadena, CA: Semiotext(e), 1997). Percy Bysshe Shelley, "Epipsychidion," in Shelley, *The Complete Poems* (New York: Random House, 2013).

102. Serge Doubrovsky, *Fils* (Paris: Librairie générale française, 1977). Gertrude Stein, *The Autobiography of Alice B. Toklas* (New York: Vintage Books, 1961). Max Cavitch, "Everybody's Autotheory," *Modern Language Quarterly*, 83.1 (March 2022).

103. Donald Winnicott, *The Child, the Family, and the Out-side World* (London: Penguin, 1973). Lauren Oyler, "For Goodness' Sake: The Self-Conscious Drama of Morality in Contemporary Fiction," *Bookforum*, Summer 2020.

104. Netta Yerushalmy, interview by Jack Halberstam, *BOMB Magazine*, 151 (Spring 2020).

105. Hannah Arendt, *The Life of the Mind: Thinking* (New York: Harcourt Brace, 1981). Augustine, *The Retractions* (Washington, DC: Catholic University of America Press, 1999). Nietzsche, *Ecce Homo.*

107. Michel Foucault, *Discipline and Punish: The Birth of the Prison* (New York: Vintage Books, 1995).

108. Guntrip, *Schizoid Phenomena.*

109. Fairbairn, *Psychoanalytic Studies.* Dore Ashton, *A Joseph Cornell Album* (Cambridge, MA: Da Capo, 2002). Nietzsche, *On the Genealogy of Morals.*

110. Kishik, *Wittgenstein's Form of Life.* Ludwig Wittgenstein, *Tractatus Logico-Philosophicus* (Mineola, NY: Dover, 1998). Ludwig Wittgenstein, *Philosophical Investigations* (Oxford: Blackwell, 1997). Kishik, *The Power of Life.*

111. Giorgio Agamben, *The Omnibus Homo Sacer* (Stanford, CA: Stanford University Press, 2017). Kishik, *The Manhat-*

tan Project. Walter Benjamin, *The Arcades Project* (Cambridge, MA: Belknap Press, 1999).

112. Kishik, *The Book of Shem.*

113. Kishik, *The Book of Shem.* Frieda Fromm-Reichmann, "Loneliness," *Psychiatry*, 22.1 (February 1959). Thomas Wolfe, "The Anatomy of Loneliness," in *The Complete Short Stories of Thomas Wolfe* (New York: Simon and Schuster, 1989). Baruch Spinoza, *Ethics* (Indianapolis, IN: Hackett, 1992). Moshe Sakal, "De Beauvoir and Sartre on the Kibbutz," *World Literature Today*, 92.4 (July 2018). Maggie Nelson, *The Argonauts* (Minneapolis, MN: Graywolf, 2016).

114. Lee Edelman, *No Future* (Durham, NC: Duke University Press, 2004). Walter Benjamin, "On the Concept of History," in Benjamin, *Selected Writings*, 4 vols (Cambridge, MA: Belknap Press, 1996–2003), IV: *1938–1940* (2003). Donald Winnicott, "From Dependence Towards Independence in the Development of the Individual," in Winnicott, *The Collected Works*, VI.

115. Karl Ove Knausgård, *My Struggle: Book Two* (New York: Farrar, Straus and Giroux, 2013). Kraus, *I Love Dick.* Nelson, *The Argonauts.* Sheila Heti, *Motherhood* (Toronto: Vintage Canada, 2019). Ben Lerner, *10:04* (New York: Farrar, Straus and Giroux, 2014). Annie Ernaux, *Happening* (New York: Seven Stories, 2001).

116. H. Gareth Gavin, *Never Was* (Cambridge: Cipher Press, 2023). Peter Sloterdijk, "Rules for the Human Zoo: A Response to the Letter of Humanism," *Environment and Planning: Society and Space*, 27.1 (2009). Jacques Derrida, *The Post Card: From Socrates to Freud and Beyond* (Chicago: University of Chicago Press, 1980).

117. Heti, *Motherhood.* Boethius, *The Consolation of Philosophy.*

118. Kishik, *The Book of Shem.* Heti, *Motherhood.*

119. Fairbairn, *Psychoanalytic Studies.*

120. J. M. Coetzee, *Disgrace* (London: Vintage, 1999). Giorgio Agamben, *What Is an Apparatus?*

121. Joakim Garff, *Søren Kierkegaard: A Biography* (Princeton, NJ: Princeton University Press, 2007). Heti, *Motherhood.* Sigmund Freud, "Mourning and Melancholia," in Freud, *On Murder, Mourning, and Melancholia* (London: Penguin, 2005).

122. Jean Laplanche, "Foundations: Towards a General Theory of Seduction," in Laplanche, *New Foundations for Psychoanalysis* (Oxford: Basil Blackwell, 1989).

126. Wittgenstein, *Culture and Value.*

127. Friedrich Nietzsche, *The Twilight of the Idols*, in *The Portable Nietzsche* (New York: Penguin, 1976).

128. Guntrip, *Schizoid Phenomena.* Proverbs 14.33. Talmud, *Bava Metzia*, 85b.2.

129. Johann Wolfgang von Goethe, *The Sorrows of Young Werther* (New York: Modern Library, 2004). Thomas Mann, "Tonio Kröger," in Mann, *Death in Venice and Other Tales* (New York: Viking, 1998). Rainer Maria Rilke, *The Notebooks of Malte Laurids Brigge* (Champaign, IL: Dalkey Archive, 2008). Ben Lerner, *Leaving the Atocha Station* (Minneapolis, IN: Coffee House Press, 2011). Sheila Heti, *How Should a Person Be?* (New York: Picador, 2013). Karl Ove Knausgård, *My Struggle: Book Five* (New York: Farrar, Straus and Giroux, 2016). Franz Kafka, *Letters to Friends, Family, and Editors* (New York: Schocken, 1977).

130. Gil Anidjar, private communication. William Shakespeare, *Hamlet* (New York: Norton, 2019).

131. Giorgio Agamben, *When the House Burns Down* (London: Seagull, 2022). Yu-jin Chang, private communication.

132. Winnicott, "Communicating and Not Communicating."

134. Please visit <https://formoflife.net>.

135. Sigmund Freud, *Civilization and its Discontents* (New York: Norton, 2010). Alex Dubilet, *The Self-Emptying Subject: Kenosis and Immanence, Medieval to Modern* (New York: Fordham University Press, 2018). Hoffmann, *The Idea of Self, East and West.* Joan Didion, *The Year of Magical Thinking* (New York: Vintage, 2007). Giorgio Agamben, *Autoritratto Nello Studio* (Milano: Nottetempo, 2017), to which this self study serves as homage.

FIGURES

BIBLIOGRAPHY

Adorno, Theodor, *Minima Moralia: Reflections from Damaged Life* (London: Verso, 2005)

Agamben, Giorgio, *Autoritratto Nello Studio* (Milano: Nottetempo, 2017)

—— "Biosecurity and Politics," in Agamben, *Where Are We Now?* (London: ERIS, 2021)

—— "The Friend," in Agamben, *What Is an Apparatus? and Other Essays* (Stanford, CA: Stanford University Press, 2009)

—— *The Idea of Prose* (Albany: State University of New York Press, 1995)

—— *Infancy and History: The Destruction of Experience* (London: Verso, 2007)

—— *The Omnibus Homo Sacer* (Stanford, CA: Stanford University Press, 2017)

—— "On the Uses and Disadvantages of Living among Specters," in Agamben, *Nudities* (Stanford, CA: Stanford University Press, 2010)

—— *The Open: Man and Animal* (Stanford, CA: Stanford University Press, 2012)

—— *Remnants of Auschwitz: The Witness and the Archive* (New York: Zone Books, 2000)

—— *Stanzas: Word and Phantasm in Western Culture* (Minneapolis: University of Minnesota Press, 1993)

—— *The Use of Bodies* (Stanford, CA: Stanford University Press, 2016)

—— "What is an Act of Creation," in Agamben, *The Fire and the Tale* (Stanford, CA: Stanford University Press, 2017)

—— *When the House Burns Down* (London: Seagull, 2022)

Ahmed, Sara, *Living a Feminist Life* (Durham, NC: Duke University Press, 2017)

Arendt, Hannah, *The Life of the Mind: Thinking* (New York: Harcourt Brace, 1981)

—— *Love and Saint Augustine* (Chicago: University of Chicago Press, 2014)

—— *The Origins of Totalitarianism* (London: Penguin, 2017)

Aristotle, *The Politics*, in *The Basic Works of Aristotle* (New York: Random House, 1941)

Ashton, Dore, *A Joseph Cornell Album* (Cambridge, MA: Da Capo, 2002)

Augustine, *Confessions* (Oxford: Oxford University Press, 1991)

—— *The Retractions* (Washington, DC: Catholic University of America Press, 1999)

Aurelius, Marcus, *Meditations* (New York: Random House, 2003)

Avedon, Richard, and James Baldwin, *Nothing Personal* (New York: Atheneum, 1964)

Azaad, Amba, "The Malignant Melancholy," *The New Inquiry,* 29 January 2018 <https://thenewinquiry.com/the-malignant-melancholy> [accessed 29 September 2022]

Baldwin, James, "Letter from a Region of My Mind," in Baldwin, *The Fire Next Time* (New York: Penguin, 1990)

Barthes, Roland, *Roland Barthes* (Berkeley: University of California Press, 1994)

Benjamin, Jessica, *Beyond Doer and Done to: Recognition Theory, Intersubjectivity and the Third* (London: Routledge, 2017)

Benjamin, Walter, *The Arcades Project* (Cambridge, MA: Belknap Press, 1999)

—— "On the Concept of History," in Benjamin, *Selected Writings*, 4 vols (Cambridge, MA: Belknap Press, 1996–2003), IV: *1938–1940* (2003)

Berlant, Lauren, *Cruel Optimism* (Durham, NC: Duke University Press, 2012)

Binswanger, Ludwig, "The Case of Lola Voss," in *Being-in-the-World: Selected Papers of Ludwig Binswanger* (New York: Basic Books, 1963)

Bishop, Claire, *Artificial Hells: Participatory Art and the Politics of Spectatorship* (London: Verso, 2012)

Bleuler, Eugen, *Dementia Praecox; or, The Group of Schizophrenias* (New York: International Universities Press, 1950)

Blumenberg, Hans, *Shipwreck with Spectator: Paradigm of a Metaphor for Existence* (Cambridge, MA: MIT Press, 2013)

Boethius, *The Consolation of Philosophy* (Cambridge, MA: Harvard University Press, 2008)

Bolk, Ludwig, "On the Problem of Anthropogenesis," *Proceedings of the Royal Academy, Amsterdam*, 29 (1926)

Butler, Judith, *Precarious Life: The Powers of Mourning and Violence* (London: Verso, 2004)

Casey, Edward S., "Being on Edge and Falling Apart," in Casey, *The World on Edge* (Bloomington: Indiana University Press, 2017)

Cavell, Stanley, *Little Did I Know: Excerpts from Memory* (Stanford, CA: Stanford University Press, 2010)

Cavitch, Max, "Everybody's Autotheory," *Modern Language Quarterly*, 83.1 (March 2022)

Coccia, Emanuele, "Reversing the New Global Monasticism," *Fall Semester*, 21 April 2020 <https://fallsemester.org/2020-1/2020/4/17/emanuele-coccia-escaping-the-global-monasticism> [accessed 22 July 2022]

Coetzee, J. M., *Disgrace* (London: Vintage, 1999)

Dalí, Salvador, *Madonna*, 1958, Metropolitan Museum of Art, New York

Dames, Nicholas, "The New Fiction of Solitude," *The Atlantic*, April 2016

Debord, Guy, *The Society of the Spectacle* (New York: Zone Books, 2012)

DeCaroli, Steven, "The Idea of Awakening: Giorgio Agamben and the Nagarjuna," *Res Publica*, 28 (2012)

Deleuze, Gilles, *The Logic of Sense* (New York: Columbia University Press, 1989)

Deleuze, Gilles, and Félix Guattari, *Anti-Oedipus: Capitalism and Schizophrenia* (London: Continuum, 1983)

—— *What Is Philosophy?* (London: Verso, 2015)

Derrida, Jacques, *The Post Card: From Socrates to Freud and Beyond* (Chicago: University of Chicago Press, 1980)

Descartes, René, *Discourse on Method and Meditations on First Philosophy* (Indianapolis, IN: Hackett, 2010)

Devereux, George, *Basic Problems of Ethnopsychiatry* (Chicago: University of Chicago Press, 1980)

Didion, Joan, *The Year of Magical Thinking* (New York: Vintage, 2007)

Doubrovsky, Serge, *Fils* (Paris: Librairie générale française, 1977)

Dubilet, Alex, *The Self-Emptying Subject: Kenosis and Immanence, Medieval to Modern* (New York: Fordham University Press, 2018)

Edelman, Lee, *No Future* (Durham, NC: Duke University Press, 2004)

Emerson, Ralph Waldo, "The American Scholar," in Emerson, *The Essential Writings* (New York: Modern Library, 2000)

Epictetus, *Discourses, Fragments, Handbook* (Oxford: Oxford University Press, 2014)

Ernaux, Annie, *Happening* (New York: Seven Stories, 2001)

Fairbairn, W. R. D., *Psychoanalytic Studies of the Personality* (London: Routledge, 1952)

—— "Synopsis of an Object-Relations Theory of the Personality," *The International Journal of Psychoanalysis*, 44.2 (1963)

Fanon, Frantz, *Black Skin, White Masks* (London: Pluto Press, 1986)

Foucault, Michel, *The Care of the Self* (New York: Vintage, 1990)

—— *Discipline and Punish: The Birth of the Prison* (New York: Vintage Books, 1995)

—— *The Government of Self and Others: Lectures at the Collège de France, 1982–1983* (London: Palgrave Macmillan, 2010)

—— "The Hermeneutics of the Subject," in Foucault, *Ethics: Subjectivity and Truth* (New York: New Press, 1997)

—— *Subjectivity and Truth: Lectures at the Collège de France, 1980–1981* (London: Palgrave, 2016)

Fournier, Lauren, *Autotheory as Feminist Practice in Art, Writing, and Criticism* (Cambridge, MA: MIT Press, 2021)

Freud, Sigmund, *Civilization and its Discontents* (New York: Norton, 2010)

—— "Mourning and Melancholia," in Freud, *On Murder, Mourning, and Melancholia* (London: Penguin, 2005)

—— "The Neuro-Psychoses of Defence," in *The Standard Edition of the Complete Psychological Works of Sigmund Freud*, 24 vols (London: Hogarth, 1953–74), III: *Early Psychoanalytic Publications (1893–1899)* (1962)

Fromm-Reichmann, Frieda, "Loneliness," *Psychiatry*, 22.1 (February 1959)

Garff, Joakim, *Søren Kierkegaard: A Biography* (Princeton, NJ: Princeton University Press, 2007)

Gavin, H. Gareth, *Never Was* (Cambridge: Cipher Press, 2023)

Goethe, Johann Wolfgang von, *The Sorrows of Young Werther* (New York: Modern Library, 2004)

Greenberg, Jay, and Stephen Mitchell, *Object Relations in Psychoanalytic Theory* (Cambridge, MA: Harvard University Press, 1983)

Guntrip, Harry, *Personal Relations Therapy* (London: Aronson, 1994)

—— *Schizoid Phenomena, Object Relations and the Self* (London: Routledge, 1992)

Halberstam, Judith, "The Anti-Social Turn in Queer Studies," *Graduate Journal of Social Science*, 5.2 (2008)

Hegel, G. W. F., *Phenomenology of Spirit* (Oxford: Oxford University Press, 1977)

Heidegger, Martin, *Being and Time* (Albany: State University of New York Press, 1996)

Heller-Roazen, Daniel, *The Inner Touch: Archaeology of a Sensation* (New York: Zone Books, 2007)

Heti, Sheila, *How Should a Person Be?* (New York: Picador, 2013)

—— *Motherhood* (Toronto: Vintage Canada, 2019)

Hoffmann, Yoel, *The Idea of Self, East and West: A Comparison between Buddhist Philosophy and the Philosophy of David Hume* (Calcutta: K.L.M, 1980)

Horney, Karen, "Resignation: the Appeal of Freedom," in Horney, *Neurosis and Human Growth: The Struggle Toward Self-Realization* (New York: Norton, 1950)

Hume, David, *The Private Correspondence of David Hume* (London: Henry Colburn, 1820)

Inwood, Brad, and Lloyd Gerson, eds, *The Stoics Reader: Selected Writings and Testimonia* (Indianapolis, IN: Hackett, 2008)

Kafka, Franz, *The Blue Octavo Notebooks* (Cambridge, MA: Exact Change, 1991)

—— "The Burrow," in Kafka, *The Complete Stories* (New York: Schocken, 1946)

—— *The Complete Novels: The Trial, America, the Castle* (London: Vintage, 2008)

—— *Letters to Friends, Family, and Editors* (New York: Schocken, 1977)

Kierkegaard, Søren, *The Concept of Irony* (Princeton, NJ: Princeton University Press, 1992)

—— *Papers and Journals* (London: Penguin, 2015)

Kishik, David, *The Book of Shem: On Genesis Before Abraham* (Stanford, CA: Stanford University Press, 2018)

—— *The Manhattan Project: A Theory of a City* (Stanford, CA: Stanford University Press, 2015)

—— *The Power of Life: Agamben and the Coming Politics* (Stanford, CA: Stanford University Press, 2011)

—— *Wittgenstein's Form of Life* (London: Continuum, 2008)

Klein, Melanie, "Notes on Some Schizoid Mechanisms," *International Journal of Psycho-Analysis*, 27 (1946)

Knausgård, Karl Ove, *My Struggle: Book Two* (New York: Farrar, Straus and Giroux, 2013)

—— *My Struggle: Book Five* (New York: Farrar, Straus and Giroux, 2016)

—— *My Struggle: Book Six* (New York: Farrar, Straus and Giroux, 2018)

Kojève, Alexandre, *Introduction to the Reading of Hegel* (Ithaca, NY: Cornell University Press, 1980)

Kraus, Chris, *I Love Dick* (Pasadena, CA: Semiotext(e), 1997)

Kretschmer, Ernst, *Physique and Character* (London: Routledge, 1999)

Lacan, Jacques, *The Object Relation: The Seminar of Jacques Lacan, Book IV* (Cambridge: Polity, 2021)

Laing, Olivia, *The Lonely City: Adventures in the Art of Being Alone* (New York: Picador, 2016)

Laing, R. D., *The Divided Self: An Existential Study in Sanity and Madness* (London: Penguin, 2010)

—— *Knots* (New York: Pantheon, 1970)

Laplanche, Jean, "Foundations: Towards a General Theory of Seduction," in Laplanche, *New Foundations for Psychoanalysis* (Oxford: Basil Blackwell, 1989)

—— "Time and the Other," in Laplanche, *Essays on Otherness* (London: Routledge, 1999)

—— "The Unfinished Copernican Revolution," in Laplanche, *Essays on Otherness*

Lebowitz, Fran, *The Fran Lebowitz Reader* (New York: Knopf, 1994)

Lerner, Ben, *10:04* (New York: Farrar, Straus and Giroux, 2014)

—— *Leaving the Atocha Station* (Minneapolis, IN: Coffee House Press, 2011)

Li, Yiyun, *Dear Friend, from My Life I Write to You in Your Life* (London: Penguin, 2018)

Lotringer, Sylvère, and David Morris, *Schizo-Culture* (Pasadena, CA: Semiotext(e), 2014)

Lukács, György, *Soul & Form* (New York: Columbia University Press, 2010)

Mann, Thomas, "Tonio Kröger," in Mann, *Death in Venice and Other Tales* (New York: Viking, 1998)

Masson, Jeffery M., "Freud and the Seduction Theory," *The Atlantic*, February 1984

Mcgushin, Edward, *Foucault's Askesis: An Introduction to the Philosophical Life* (Evanston, IL: Northwestern University Press, 2007)

Mcwilliams, Nancy, "Schizoid Personality," in McWilliams, *Psychoanalytic Diagnosis* (New York: Guilford Press, 2011)

—— "Some Thoughts about Schizoid Dynamics," *The Psychoanalytic Review*, 93.1 (2006)

Melville, Herman, "Bartleby the Scrivener," in Melville, *Billy Budd, Sailor, and Other Stories* (London: Penguin, 1985)

Miller, Jacques-Alain, "A Fantasy," *Lacanian Praxis*, 1.11 (2005)

Montaigne, Michel de, "Experience," in Montaigne, *Selected Essays* (Indianapolis, IN: Hackett, 2012)

Nancy, Jean-Luc, "Abandoned Being," in Nancy, *The Birth to Presence* (Stanford, CA: Stanford University Press, 2009)

Nelson, Maggie, *The Argonauts* (Minneapolis, MN: Graywolf, 2016)

—— *Bluets* (Seattle, WA: Wave Books, 2009)

Nietzsche, Friedrich, *The Gay Science* (Cambridge: Cambridge University Press, 2001)

—— *On the Genealogy of Morals and Ecce Homo* (New York: Vintage, 2010)

—— *The Twilight of the Idols*, in *The Portable Nietzsche* (New York: Penguin, 1976)

Oyler, Lauren, "For Goodness' Sake: The Self-Conscious Drama of Morality in Contemporary Fiction," *Bookforum*, Summer 2020

Pascal, Blaise, *Pensées* (London: Penguin, 1995)

Piper, Adrian, "Food for the Spirit (1971)," in Piper, *Out of Order, Out of Sight* (Cambridge, MA: MIT Press, 1996)

Plato, *Alcibiades*, in *Plato: Complete Works* (Indianapolis, IN: Hackett, 1997)

Preciado, Paul B., "Learning from the Virus," *Artforum*, May/June 2020

—— *Pornotopia: An Essay on Playboy's Architecture and Biopolitics* (New York: Zone Books, 2014)

—— *Testo Junkie: Sex, Drugs, and Biopolitics in the Pharmacopornographic Era* (New York: The Feminist Press, 2013)

Rilke, Rainer Maria, *The Notebooks of Malte Laurids Brigge* (Champaign, IL: Dalkey Archive, 2008)

Rilke, Rainer Maria, and Lou Andreas-Salomé, *Rilke and Andreas-Salomé: A Love Story in Letters* (New York: Norton, 2008)

Ruti, Mari, *The Ethics of Opting Out: Queer Theory's Defiant Subjects* (New York: Columbia University Press, 2017)

Sacks, Oliver, "The Disembodied Lady," in Sacks, *The Man Who Mistook His Wife for a Hat* (London: Picador, 2015)

Sakal, Moshe, "De Beauvoir and Sartre on the Kibbutz," *World Literature Today*, 92.4 (July 2018)

Sartre, Jean-Paul, *No Exit* (New York: Vintage, 1989)

Sass, Louis, "Deep Disquietudes: Reflections on Wittgenstein as Antiphilosopher," in *Wittgenstein: Biography and Philosophy*, ed. by James C. Klagge (Cambridge: Cambridge University Press, 2001)

—— *Madness and Modernism: Insanity in the Light of Modern Art, Literature, and Thought* (Oxford: Oxford University Press, 2017)

—— *The Paradoxes of Delusion: Wittgenstein, Schreber, and the Schizophrenic Mind* (Ithaca, NY: Cornell University Press, 1994)

Schopenhauer, Arthur, "Similes, Parables, and Fables," in Schopenhauer, *Parerga and Paralipomena* (Oxford: Clarendon, 2010)

Seinfeld, Jeffrey, *The Empty Core: An Object Relations Approach to the Psychotherapy of the Schizoid Personality* (Northvale, NJ: Aronson, 1991)

Shakespeare, William, *Hamlet* (New York: Norton, 2019)

Shelley, Percy Bysshe, "Epipsychidion," in Shelley, *The Complete Poems* (New York: Random House, 2013)

Sherman, Nancy, *Stoic Warriors: The Ancient Philosophy Behind the Military Mind* (Oxford: Oxford University Press, 2005)

Sloterdijk, Peter, *In the World Interior of Capital: For a Philosophical Theory of Globalization* (Cambridge: Polity, 2014)

—— "Rules for the Human Zoo: A Response to the Letter of Humanism," *Environment and Planning: Society and Space*, 27.1 (2009)

Spinoza, Baruch, *Ethics* (Indianapolis, IN: Hackett, 1992)

Stagg, Natasha, *Sleeveless: Fashion, Image, Media, New York 2011–2019* (Pasadena, CA: Semiotext(e), 2017)

Stein, Gertrude, *The Autobiography of Alice B. Toklas* (New York: Vintage Books, 1961)

Stolorow, Robert, *Faces in a Cloud: Intersubjectivity in Personality Theory* (Northvale, NJ: Aronson, 1993)

Suwa, Mami, and Kunifumi Suzuki, "The Phenomenon of 'Hikikomori' (Social Withdrawal) and the Socio-cultural Situation in Japan Today," *Journal of Psychopathology*, 19 (2013)

Triest, Yossi, "Corona-Time Notes: The Virus of Horror," *The Tavistock Institute*, March 2020 <https://tavinstitute.org/projects/corona-time-notes-the-virus-of-horror> [accessed 2 October 2022]

Turing, Alan, "Computing Machinery and Intelligence," *Mind*, 59 (October 1950)

Turkle, Sherry, *Alone Together: Why We Expect More from Technology and Less from Each Other* (New York: Basic Books, 2017)

Wallace, David Foster, "E Unibus Pluram," in Wallace, *A Supposedly Fun Thing I'll Never Do Again* (New York: Little, Brown and Company, 1997)

Watkin, William, *Agamben and Indifference* (London: Rowman & Littlefield, 2014)

Weil, Simone, *First and Last Notebooks* (Oxford: Oxford University Press, 1970)

Whitman, Walt, "Song of Myself," in Whitman, *Poetry and Prose*, ed. by Justin Kaplan (New York: Library of America, 1982)

Wilderson, Frank B., *Afropessimism* (New York: Liverlight, 2020)

Winnicott, Donald W., *The Child, the Family, and the Outside World* (London: Penguin, 1973)

—— "Communicating and Not Communicating," in *The Collected Works of D. W. Winnicott,* 12 vols (Oxford: Oxford University Press, 2016), VI: 1960–63

—— "Creativity and its Origins," in Winnicott, *Playing and Reality* (New York: Routledge, 2005)

—— "Ego Integration and Child Development," in Winnicott, *The Maturational Processes and the Facilitating Environment* (Abingdon: Routledge, 2018)

—— "Fear of Breakdown," *International Review of Psycho-Analysis*, 1.1–2 (1974)

—— "From Dependence Towards Independence in the Development of the Individual," in Winnicott, *The Collected Works*, VI

—— "The Theory of the Parent-Infant Relationship," in Winnicott, *The Maturational Processes*

—— "Transitional Objects and Transitional Phenomena," in Winnicott, *Playing and Reality*

—— "The Use of an Object and Relating through Identification," in Winnicott, *Playing and Reality*

Wittgenstein, Ludwig, *Culture and Value* (Chicago: University of Chicago Press, 2006)

—— *Philosophical Investigations* (Oxford: Blackwell, 1997)

—— *Private Notebooks: 1914–1916* (New York: Liveright, 2022)

—— *Tractatus Logico-Philosophicus* (Mineola, NY: Dover, 1998)

Wolfe, Thomas, "The Anatomy of Loneliness," in *The Complete Short Stories of Thomas Wolfe* (New York: Simon and Schuster, 1989)

Yerushalmy, Netta, interview by Jack Halberstam, *BOMB Magazine*, 151 (Spring 2020)

Young-Bruehl, Elizabeth, *Hannah Arendt: For Love of the World* (New Haven, CT: Yale University Press, 1982)

Ziprin, Lionel, *Songs for Schizoid Siblings* (New York: The Song Cave, 2017)

Žižek, Slavoj, *How to Read Lacan* (New York: Norton, 2007)